ONCE A LAND OF BIRDS

ALSO BY MAGI NAMS

in the *Cry of the Kiwi* trilogy:

This Dark Sheltering Forest

Tang of the Tasman Sea

ABOUT THE AUTHOR

MAGI NAMS studied zoology at the University of Alberta and high arctic plant ecology at Dalhousie University before turning to writing. She is passionate about exploring the natural world and has published dozens of nature articles in the children's magazine *Ranger Rick*. The ten months she and her family lived in New Zealand became the subject of her *Cry of the Kiwi* trilogy. She lives in Nova Scotia, Canada, and is working on her next book, *Red Continent*, about a year of birding, bushwalking, and exploring in Australia. Visit her website at **www.maginams.ca.**

AUTHOR'S NOTE

The places, events, and people in this book are real. Some individuals' names and identifying characteristics have been changed to protect their privacy.

ONCE A LAND
OF BIRDS

Cry of the Kiwi:
A Family's New Zealand Adventure

Book 1: South Island I

MAGI NAMS

For more information, contact Magi Nams at **www.maginams.ca**

Library and Archives Canada Cataloguing in Publication
Nams, Margorie Linda Nietfeld, author
    Cry of the kiwi : a family's New Zealand adventure / Magi Nams.

Includes bibliographical references and index.
Contents: book 1. South Island I : Once a land of birds
Issued in print and electronic formats.
ISBN 978-0-9937767-0-0 (bk. 1 : pbk.).--ISBN 978-0-9937767-3-1 (bk. 1 : pdf)

    1. Nams, Margorie Linda Nietfeld--Travel--New Zealand. 2. New Zealand--Description and travel. 3. Natural history--New Zealand. 4. Ecology--New Zealand. 5. Home schooling. I. Title. II. Title: Once a land of birds.

DU413.N34 2015   919.304412   C2015-902223-1
                                             C2015-902224-X

Editing by Pat Thomas
Cover and interior design by Magi Nams
Photography and map by Vilis and Magi Nams

Permission to quote brief passages from the following works is gratefully acknowledged:
Penguin Books – *A History of New Zealand* by Keith Sinclair, on p. 98
Keri Hulme – *The Bone People*, on p. 122
Auckland University Press – *Waitangi and Indigenous Rights: Revolution, Law, and Legitimation* by F. M. (Jock) Brookfield, on p. 155
Janet Frame Literary Trust – *Owls Do Cry*, on p. 204

If a permission has been inadvertently overlooked, the author and publisher apologizes and will be happy to make a correction.

FOR MY MOTHER, MARY NIETFELD, AND
IN MEMORY OF MY FATHER, HENRY NIETFELD

BOTH GAVE ME A LOVE FOR THE LAND

CONTENTS

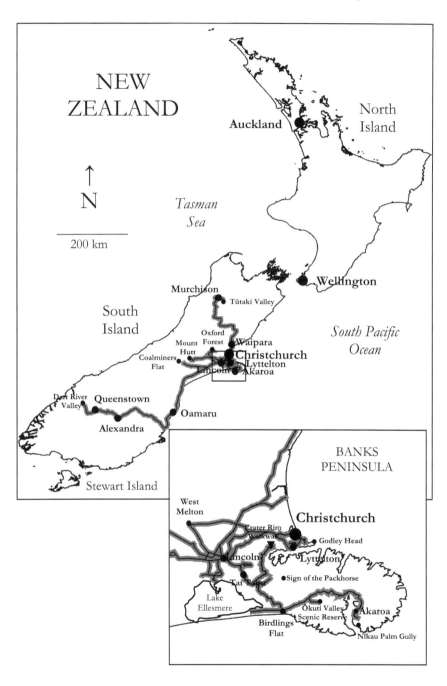

PREFACE

ALL MY life, I'd dreamed of travelling to far-away countries to hike through landscapes inhabited by exotic animals and plants I'd seen in *National Geographic* or on television. In the year 2000, my dream came true when my husband, two sons, and I left our home in rural Nova Scotia, Canada, and spent ten months in New Zealand.

Our sojourn on the far side of the world was our first extended absence from Canada. As we made our final preparations to travel, we were filled with excitement at the prospect of hiking on volcanoes and exploring tangled rainforests (maybe we'd even see a kiwi bird!) but we also had qualms. Would the tenant renting our house take good care of it? Would our cats remember us when we returned? Would we like New Zealand? Would the kids make friends? Would we be safe?

We didn't pack much to take with us: some clothes, a laptop, binoculars, skates, sleeping bags, and a box of school books. We arrived in New Zealand wide-eyed and unsure of what to expect. Ten months later we returned to Canada inspired and broadened in ways I'd never imagined. Our New Zealand adventure opened our eyes to the world and helped shape who we are.

The *Cry of the Kiwi* trilogy began as observations I scribbled in small notebooks during my family's travels and outdoor adventures in New Zealand, and entries in our homeschooling journal. While living there, I roughed out a few "NZ stories" intended for a private memoir. After our return to Canada, a persistent internal voice told me I should write more of our adventures and turn them into a book.

As happens in life, other responsibilities intruded, with the result that *Cry of the Kiwi* was fourteen years in the making and became one story in three parts: *Once a Land of Birds, This Dark Sheltering Forest,* and *Tang of the Tasman Sea.*

As our New Zealand adventure drew to a close in 2001, I realized that the heart of that country lay as much in its people as in its riveting landscapes and intriguing flora and fauna. Thank you, New Zealand, for the adventure of a lifetime. Perhaps my family's story will inspire others to go adventuring far from home.

Kia ora,
Magi Nams

ACKNOWLEDGEMENTS

WITHOUT THE assistance and encouragement of many people, this book would not be in your hands. Monica Graham offered insightful suggestions for an early draft and instilled in me the belief that my family adventure story could succeed. The diverse and thoughtful comments provided by beta readers Betty Hodgson, Leanne Erickson, Nikki Figueiredo, and Vilis Nams encouraged me and enabled me to polish an advanced draft. Editor Pat Thomas transformed my book dream into a clear and consistent manuscript and discerned that *Cry of the Kiwi* was really three books, not one.

In New Zealand, Christchurch City Libraries staff provided me with helpful contacts and answered numerous questions. Staff at the Māori Language Commission macronized Māori place names for me. Numerous Kiwis offered my family generous hospitality and friendship during our time in their beautiful country – my sincere gratitude to you all! Thanks also to the individuals who allowed me to include their true identities in my story, and special thanks to Andrea and Andy for giving us a home before we found a home.

Last but never least, loving thanks to my husband, Vilis, who supported me throughout this project and rescued me from numerous computer dilemmas. And hugs to my sons, Dainis and Jānis, who didn't balk at allowing me to share their roles in our New Zealand adventure with the world.

.

PROLOGUE

Spring, 2000

I'M UP early every morning; a natural early riser. I tend our dozen laying hens, roosters, and guinea fowl in the chicken coop and listen for songbirds that have returned to the meadows and forests of Ravenhill, my family's rural property in northern Nova Scotia. Birding is one of my passions. Another is exploring the natural world and learning about its inhabitants.

When the chicken chores are done, I put on my sneakers and run or walk roads near my home. I'm invigorated by fresh air, exercise, and the wonders of the world around me. My spirit soars as I tread beneath the canopy of mature hemlock trees whose branches arch over my access road like the roof of a cathedral. It's in the presence of such natural beauty that I see God's amazing power and creativity.

When I return to the house, I sweep floors before preparing breakfast for my husband, Vilis, and our sons, Dainis and Jānis. The boys set and clear the table, and Vilis washes the dishes before leaving for work at the Nova Scotia Agricultural College, where he's a professor in the Environmental Sciences Department. Dainis and Jānis feed their cats Blotchy and Baby and collect eggs from the hens (A note on pronunciations: Vilis rhymes with Phyllis, Magi sounds like Maggie, Dainis [DINE-is], and Jānis [YAWN-is]).

At 7:30 a.m. on weekdays, I begin my sons' homeschooling day by reading aloud to them for thirty minutes, as Vilis does when he teaches the boys one day a week. We choose classic children's books, historical fiction, fun reads, or non-fiction outdoor adventure books. We've had "reading time" ever since Dainis and Jānis were babies. The four of us enjoy the bond that sharing literature creates, as well as the exposure to real and imaginary worlds far beyond our daily lives.

After reading time, Dainis and Jānis complete school assignments at the kitchen table or in the living room or on the kitchen floor in front of the wood stove. It doesn't matter to me where the work gets done, as long as it gets done. Sometimes our schooling flows smoothly, and sometimes there are tears and complaints and grumblings. The boys set high standards for themselves and don't like to make mistakes: the apples have fallen close to the tree in that regard. Every day, we do stretches and calisthenics to shake off brain drain and restore enthusiasm, and the boys play our piano. As a special music project, our family sings with the local choral group each week.

Our schooling time ends at noon or 1:00 p.m., after which I record the day's work in our homeschooling journal and plan the next day's assignments. The boys have free time for the rest of the day. Blocks of the remaining time are taken up with extracurricular activities: piano lessons, swimming lessons, spring baseball, 4-H, Cubs and Scouts, wood carving lessons for Dainis, figure skating lessons for Jānis.

Our days are *very* full and sometimes too hectic. The calendar on the kitchen wall is cluttered with lessons and events. This spring is particularly busy, with added commitments: heritage fair, music festival, piano exams, choral concerts. Because I'm the parent at home, I drive my sons to many of their extracurricular activities and assist them with organizing their projects. I encourage them in their sports and piano studies and volunteer with the local Scouting organization and skating club. It would be fair to say that my life revolves around my children.

Yet, part of me rebels at the total dedication required. Like most mothers, I'm proud of my kids. However, I'm often exhausted and restless, sometimes resentful. I have so little time to explore the world around me, although as a family, we try to fit in a hike or paddle on weekends. And I have so little time to write, certainly not every day. I squeeze in a magazine article now and then, but my book projects are constantly interrupted. I know this lack of time is, in part, of my own making, since I chose to homeschool my sons and support their many activities, which they generally love (less so, the singing).

And there are the demands of everyday life. I bake bread. I cook slow food. Many of our meals include meats, vegetables, and fruits Vilis and I have produced, a task that requires time and effort. With spring's arrival, I tidy the yard and weed my beloved flowerbeds, anticipating their summer beauty. And like most other mothers, I do many menial tasks. I clean house. I wash clothes.

Sometimes I wonder if, in giving so much so much of my time to my children, I've let myself down. What happened to my dream of travelling the world and seeing exotic landscapes, plants, and animals? I studied biology for seven years in university. Part of me still wants to incorporate biology, or at least natural history, into my life. And part of me still wants a big travel adventure, a glorious trip somewhere far away, where I can walk beneath the canopies of unknown trees and identify exotic birds. Where the boys can learn about a foreign country...not for a few days, but for weeks or months. Yet, we're not wealthy people. Vilis's salary could never cover the cost of a trip like that.

There is one hope. Vilis has applied for a year-long leave from the college and for a fellowship to do ecological research in New Zealand. In the midst of my hectic and sometimes frazzled existence, my heart leaps at the possibility that we could go, that we could leave all our commitments here behind and have that adventure, that freedom to explore. Repeatedly, I caution myself to not get my hopes up. The application for the leave could fall through. The fellowship could be denied.

Life continues. I teach, drive, cook, bake, garden, feed chickens, run beneath tall trees, all the while wondering…

Vilis's application for a leave is approved. He and I look deep into each other's eyes, seeing the dream take form, like an embryo.

Life continues. I teach, drive, cook, bake, garden, feed chickens, run beneath tall trees. And I yearn. I yearn toward a positive reply from New Zealand. I pray for it with the intensity that one prays for a gift of healing.

On May 23, Vilis tells me that he's received a reply.

My mind and body tense, afraid. Afraid the dream will die.

 "I got the fellowship."

His words splinter my fear into joy, into unbounded excitement loosed from months of restraint. I shout with happiness and wrap my arms around him. We are going! We are really going!

My husband has delivered my dream.

ONCE A LAND OF BIRDS

August 9, 2000

ORANGE STREAKS flare against the night like a beckoning light at the end of the world. I stare through the window at waning darkness while my husband, Vilis, and sons, Dainis and Jānis, sleep onboard the Air New Zealand jet. A strip of cloud below the jet looks like thick smoke, tinged with the colour of ripe muskmelon. Through gaps in the cloud, I see steel-blue waves like beaten metal, and brown peaks like the humps of stampeding bison. A thrill runs through me. *This is it!* These are my first glimpses of Nieuw Zeeland (so named by Dutch geographers for their coastal province of Zeeland). To the Māori, whose ancestors arrived from Polynesia centuries before the Dutch explorer Abel Tasman sailed in search of a southern continent in 1642, this is Aotearoa, "Land of the Long White Cloud."[1]

At 5:00 a.m., a lingering darkness cloaks Auckland International Airport. Groggy from jetlag after flying half way around the world, my family trudges through New Zealand Customs. We're detained by a sniffer dog, a beagle who's detected the scent of fruit emanating from my daypack. If I had any fruit, it would have been a contravention of New Zealand's strict biosecurity regulations intended to prevent pests and diseases from entering the country,[2] however I ate the last dried apricot somewhere over the Pacific Ocean. We're released from the dog's inspection and follow directions that lead us through the airport and beyond its doors. The caress of warm air in the southern winter startles us.

"Look! There's a *palm* tree!" Jānis's voice is filled with wonder.

Despite our weariness, the sight of those gracefully curved, exotic leaves sparks excitement in us. We're four Canadians 18 000 kilometres away from home (an old farm in Nova Scotia) where palm trees definitely do not grow outdoors!

This is why we came. This is why we left the familiarity of Nova Scotia for the newness of New Zealand. We had a need to explore a part of the world far away, to see new plants and animals and landscapes, to seek new adventures and feel new experiences jolt our senses and expand our horizons. For years, as a homeschooling parent, I'd wanted to live with my husband and kids in a foreign country. Such an adventure would be the ultimate field trip. As the only ecologist on staff at the Nova Scotia Agricultural College, Vilis had for years looked forward to taking a leave to focus exclusively on his research, with no teaching responsibilities. When the New Zealand possibility arose, he and I leapt at the chance. And our sons? Jānis radiated excitement at the prospect of travel adventures. Dainis was torn between the contentment of remaining in Nova Scotia with his beloved home, friends, and LEGO, and the desire for new experiences.

Those new experiences start now, and it's Vilis's research that's made them possible. We've come to New Zealand because of an animal Kiwi conservationists wish didn't exist in their country: the stoat. A stoat is a kind of weasel. It's been declared public enemy number one of New Zealand's native birds,[3] particularly this country's national icon and unofficial symbol, the kiwi. You know the kiwi: dumpy and flightless, almost blind, and with a long beak like a poker. It's the reason New Zealanders are colloquially called "Kiwis." All five kiwi species face extinction, and stoats, which prey on kiwi chicks, are one of the main threats to kiwi survival.[4] This is where Vilis, who has experience live-trapping and radio-tracking weasels and other predatory mammals in Canada, enters the picture. He'll assume a short-term position with Landcare Research, a government agency that studies and manages terrestrial ecosystems. His research will be aimed at helping to rid New Zealand of stoats.

THE KIWI'S ARCH ENEMY

The stoat story in New Zealand is one of good intentions gone wrong with devastating results. Stoats (*Mustela erminea*) are slender brown weasels with white bellies and black-tipped tails. Agile carnivores, they're native to Northern Hemisphere countries where they hunt rodents, birds, rabbits, and hares. In 1884, English colonists brought stoats to New Zealand to try to control exploding populations of rabbits that were earlier introduced for sport hunting. Since New Zealand has no native terrestrial mammalian carnivores, the idea was to bring some in from elsewhere to deal with the rabbits. The stoats spread throughout New Zealand and did indeed hunt rabbits, however, they also killed vast numbers of native birds and now threaten the survival of New Zealand's beloved kiwi.[5]

As we stand in the warm Auckland darkness staring at a palm tree, I feel my family's horizons stretch. What adventures will the next ten-and-a-half months bring? For one of those months, Dainis, Jānis, and I will help Vilis live-trap and radio-track stoats at a research site in the Tongariro Forest Conservation Area on North Island, the northernmost half of this country. During the remainder of our sojourn, we'll be based near the Landcare Research branch in Lincoln, a township twenty kilometres southwest of Christchurch in the South Island province of Canterbury. There, as a family, we'll embark on a homeschooling and outdoor adventure odyssey intended to immerse us in New Zealand's history, culture, landscapes, flora, and fauna. As for me personally, I have three goals for my time in New Zealand: lots of hiking, lots of birding, and lots of writing.

We've been fortunate to receive the travel and educational opportunity of a lifetime, and I plan to make the most of every minute.

A blue line painted on damp pavement directs us to the domestic terminal for our flight to Christchurch, New Zealand's third largest city after Auckland and Wellington and the largest on South Island.[6] Blessedly brief, this flight is the last leg of our half-way-around-the-world journey.

As we approach our destination, the pilot announces a temperature of two degrees below freezing, much colder than the balmy air we experienced in Auckland three hours earlier and 750 kilometres northward. Below us, Christchurch is shrouded in ice fog beneath clear skies and sunshine. The Canterbury Plain surrounding it sparkles with frost and is a patchwork of pastures and fields bordered by tall, precisely trimmed hedges the likes of which we've never seen before. *Intriguing.*

In the airport, we're met by Andrea Byrom, an anxious-looking brunette holding a sign with Vilis's name on it. She smiles with relief when she spots my husband. Andrea first met Vilis at a zoology conference two years ago and has been his New Zealand contact for the past year. She's supplied him with maps and documents and has coordinated details to enable him to assume his position with Landcare Research. Vilis will collaborate with Andrea and other ecologists in the Vertebrate Pest Management Unit in their efforts to eradicate stoats.

Vilis grins and makes introductions. "Hello, Andrea! This is Magi. And this is Dainis, who's twelve, and Jānis, who's nine."

Our sons lean against me, almost speechless with shyness and fatigue. Beneath the thick fringes of their mushroom haircuts, their eyes are weary. It's been a long haul, first by train from Nova Scotia to Toronto, and then by jet to Los Angeles, Auckland, and Christchurch. I greet Andrea warmly, and Dainis and Jānis add quiet hellos.

We load our luggage into Andrea's SUV, and she drives us to her home in West Melton, a quiet rural locale comprised of small holdings and many pastures filled with sheep. Throughout the drive, the boys and I strive to follow her lilting accent, which to our ears tilts vowels and consonants in intriguing ways. She turns into a driveway next to a bright yellow mailbox, and we catch our first glimpse of her cement-block house. Its three-part layout incorporates large windows throughout. Cedar posts support a grey metal roof that overhangs a carport and veranda.

Inside, Andrea gives us a quick tour, and we carry our luggage upstairs to the airy guest rooms we'll occupy. She and her husband have graciously offered us accommodation until we arrange to rent a house.

At 9:00 a.m. (only an hour after arriving on South Island) Vilis prepares to accompany Andrea to the Landcare Research branch in Lincoln to put in his first day of work. He's keen to meet his new colleagues.

Andrea turns to me, her eyes concerned. "What will you do all day?"

We are, after all, strangers in a strange land.

I say cheerfully, "We'll explore your yard and go for a walk."

"But you won't know where you're going."

"We'll keep turning left to form a loop. Will that work?"

"Yes, it should."

In Andrea's yard, my sons and I discover daffodils that will soon flower, and numerous ornamental shrubs, some blossoming in the late southern winter (New Zealand's seasons are the opposite to

Canada's. Here, winter spans June, July, and August; spring spans September, October, and November; summer spans December, January, and February; and autumn spans March, April, and May.)

Later, sunshine and warm afternoon temperatures lure us outdoors again, and we stroll along quiet country roads with narrow paved shoulders and wide grassy verges. We become accustomed to the sight of vehicles travelling on the left side of the road and practice the basic Kiwi survival technique of checking for traffic first from our right rather than our left.

As we walk, our eager eyes are greeted by a wealth of unfamiliar vegetation. We recognize pine, cedar, and Lombardi poplar in some of the sheared hedges that tower eight to ten metres and edge paddocks with clean, straight lines. Sheep, which we were expecting ("SHEEP NEXT 1200 KM," according to a tourist souvenir sticker I bought at the airport), and a surprising number of blanketed horses graze in pastures green with grass, even in winter. We walk past a lone sheep tethered at the roadside and spot birds, some familiar and some new to us: mallards, house sparrows, starlings, a dead European goldfinch at the roadside, several spur-winged plovers cackling in a pasture. Again and again, my sons and I laugh and exclaim with excitement as we absorb our new surroundings.

At last, weary from jetlag, we turn left for the fourth time onto what should be the last leg of the loop back to Andrea's house. And that's when my left-turn plan begins to unravel. Much sooner than I expect, we encounter another intersection, where we also turn left and then hesitate. Nothing on this road looks familiar, as it should by now, since I believe we drove this route from the airport to Andrea's house. With dismay, I realize I don't know Andrea's street address.

So much for my common sense. The novelty of our

surroundings and my jetlag-induced mental wooziness enticed me away from Andrea's yard before I checked her house number and the name of the road on which she lives. As a result, I have no idea exactly where we are. Panic sweeps through me.

"What will we do?" Dainis asks. His blue eyes are anxious, his brow furrowed. Beside him, Jānis stares silently up at me, his green eyes reflecting his fatigue. The three of us droop in the winter sun, exhausted and 18 000 kilometres from home. *Pull yourself together.* I cast about for solutions to our dilemma and come up with a single fail-proof method to find Andrea's home. I tell the boys, "We'll go back the way we came. That will work." I look at their tired faces, mentally kicking myself. "I'm sorry."

Periodically, my kids astonish me with their stamina, their sheer determination, and their trust in me. This is one of those times. Dainis nods, and without complaint, he and Jānis retrace their steps, ever slower and more weary. I hold Jānis's hand and tug him along. We no longer notice the unusual plants and birds. Instead, we look only for the next intersection and the bright yellow mailbox.

"There it is!" Dainis shouts in relief.

He and Jānis crash into bed at 4:00 p.m., shivering with cold in a house built without central heating, as most New Zealand houses are. A Kiwi student Vilis met in Nova Scotia, who one day mistakenly dressed in shorts before stepping out into a winter day's cold and snow, explained that New Zealanders decide how much clothing to wear *outside* their homes based on the temperature *inside* their homes.

Dusk arrives at 5:30 p.m., hours earlier than the summer twilight we left behind in Canada. Vilis returns from Landcare with Andrea in a 1985 Ford Sierra station wagon he bought for eight hundred dollars. No doubt it was the car's bright blue colour that prompted the former owner to name it "the Blue Bomb." Soon after their arrival, Andrea's husband Andy Kliskey, a dark-eyed, muscular, slow-spoken geography professor who works at the University of Canterbury, rides up on his bicycle.

Vilis and I attempt to wake the boys for supper, but exhaustion has claimed them. We struggle against our own jetlag as we join Andrea and Andy for lasagne at a massive wood table that's as much a piece of art as a functional surface. Our hosts are incredibly welcoming, yet we can only prop our eyes open until 8:00 p.m. We apologize and stumble to bed, shivering with cold like Dainis and Jānis. As we gradually ease into warmth beneath our duvet, I realize my thoughts are utterly disjointed. It's as though the long flight over the Pacific Ocean and across the International Date Line stole more than just a day from my life.

August 10

"LOOK AT the gulls!" Jānis exclaims. He and Dainis reach for the sky and laugh.

We're in the midst of wings. Like graceful white crosses, red-billed gulls hang in brilliant blue sky, with their slender, angled wings outspread. Buoyed by a northwest wind, the gulls hover above and around us. They dive for bits of bread tossed into the air by a fellow beach walker. The same strong wind that supports the gulls lifts powdery beige sand from Sumner Beach and blows it in long, shifting fingers past our ankles. Although the wind is cool, the sun feels close and hot on our faces. Offshore, the Pacific Ocean pounds frothing waves onto the sand. We delight in the hovering gulls and laugh at the magic of their wings floating past our faces. Our souls swell along with the fierce wind and pounding surf.

It's been two months since Vilis received confirmation of funding for a one-year leave from the college, and here we are today, stretching our legs on Sumner Beach as we reconnoitre Christchurch and its surrounds, looking to find an area in which we'd like to rent a house. Yesterday's exhaustion is forgotten. The boys were awake at 4:00 a.m. and giggled with excitement before Vilis lovingly shushed them and told them to go back to sleep.

After breakfast, while we drove to Lincoln and then to Christchurch, Vilis acquainted himself with the station wagon's quirks and driving on the left side of the road.

Christchurch seemed to be a city of the plain when we entered it from the southwest. I'm amazed that it also encompasses this beach and adjacent cliffs to which houses cling. Chilled by the wind, but keen to see more, we drive past the cliffs and up into the volcanic Port Hills at the city's southeast edge. Summit Road's narrow pavement rides the hills' crests, hugs sharply angled slopes, and doubles back on itself in switchbacks. Again and again, I clench my hands and stare down plunging hillsides while Vilis drives coolly on. Surprisingly, the hills provide pasture for sheep and cattle that have grazed new green grasses and avoided densely twigged shrubs and tawny tussocks (tall tougher grass that grows in individual clumps).

We laugh in surprise at the first cyclists we see labouring upward on Summit Road. "Maybe they're training for competition," I suggest. Our surprise gives way to admiration when we see more cyclists, as well as runners, pushing hard against gravity on their way up the steep inclines and then flying with it on the way down.

"Pull over," I tell Vilis, and from a scenic pull-off alongside Summit Road, we gaze at a panorama that spans half South Island's breadth. Below us, to the north, lie pale Sumner Beach and the glinting grid of Christchurch streets. To the north, southwest, and west of the city, brown and green farm fields create a patchwork that covers the Canterbury Plain. West of the plain, the snow-capped Southern Alps rear against the sky, enticing us with their high peaks. Closer to hand, the tawny Port Hills drop to the town of Lyttelton and the vivid turquoise of Lyttelton Harbour, the drowned crater of ancient Lyttelton Volcano on which we stand as we gaze out over Canterbury.

Our intense travel preparations seem to fade to another world. The packing and cleaning. All the arranging. Before departure from Canada, our lives stood ready, like a twisting curve of dominos that, with a single tap, would plunge us headlong into high-speed final preparations. When the tap came in the form of the confirmation letter, the dominos began to work their magic. Vilis applied for passports and visas. I cancelled a canoeing course for Dainis and summer figure skating school for Jānis and then made arrangements so my sons could pursue Scouting and skating in New Zealand. I bought a new pair of skates for myself, and Vilis encouraged me to look into the possibility of adult skating lessons at the rink where Jānis would be skating, as a break from my responsibilities as mother and teacher. In the final two weeks before departure, we rushed through more harried preparations: sending additional documentation to receive visas; advertising for someone to rent our house; saying farewell to friends; attending the last of the kids' activities; cleaning the house; and packing our belongings into what seemed like an endless pile of boxes for storage. None of that matters now.

We're here, in a land shaped by molten lava, ice, and the slow, upward-buckling collision of two sections of the Earth's crust known as the Australian (or Indo-Australian) and Pacific Tectonic Plates.[7] Today, New Zealand is still scraped by glaciers, shivers with earthquakes, and spurts boiling mud, geysers, and volcanic lava and ash. It's a small country: just a slender pair of major islands, the North and South Islands, plus Stewart Island and a scattering of smaller islands, all of which stretch 1 500 kilometres in a gentle, westward arc.[8] However, as we see in the magnificent view from Summit Road, this small country is packed with diverse landscapes that rub up against each other in convenient proximity for travellers. It's a gift I can't wait to unwrap.

We would explore more, but already the sun has dropped behind western clouds. Its departure brings a moody dusk. Yesterday we were so exhausted, it seemed that darkness would never fall. Today as we drive out of the hills and back to West Melton's farming country, darkness arrives startlingly early.

We left Canada in the midst of long summer days and arrived in Christchurch during the last month of New Zealand's winter. To our Canadian sensibilities, the temperatures don't feel like winter, although morning frost covered the ground yesterday and today. The landscape, with the exception of the snow-covered Southern Alps, doesn't look like the winters to which we're accustomed, wherein deciduous trees are bare of leaves and the ground is usually covered with snow. Instead, lawns and pastures are green, and many trees and shrubs are in full blossom.

Yet, the sun does not lie. Here, at approximately forty-four degrees south latitude, it rises and sets with what are definitely winter hours. We've changed seasons in midstream. Not only that. Here in the Southern Hemisphere, the winter sun is low in the north rather than south, and stars are unfamiliar in the night sky. The disorientation that these differences and jetlag have produced leave me feeling a vague sense of loss, as though a familiar and well-loved possession has gone missing.

August 11

STRONG WINDS blast out of the south this morning, their chill carried 2 400 kilometres northward from Antarctica. Dainis, Jānis, and I bundle up in jackets, gloves, and baseball caps and walk West Melton's rural roadsides.

"We're not going to have to walk all the way around *twice* today, are we?" Jānis asks, laughing, and I assure him that we won't. From a road map, I learned about the crescent that caused our confusion two days ago. Had we known we'd almost completed the loop, I wouldn't have opted to retrace our steps. Instead, my cautious decision transformed what was intended to be a pleasant stroll into a ten-kilometre endurance test!

"I hope sheepie's there," Dainis comments, as we try to remember where we saw the lone sheep tethered at the roadside.

While we stroll, we marvel at West Melton's small manicured farms with their neat fields and tall hedges. The fields are roughly equivalent in size to farm fields in northern Nova Scotia, but miniscule in comparison with the huge grain farms and ranches of the Canadian prairies, where I grew up. Two days ago when my sons and I first explored, I guessed that the tall hedges must be for protection from winter winds. Later on that walk, we met and chatted with a friendly local couple who explained that Kiwi farmers grow the hedges as protection from *summer* winds – strong, warm northwesterlies. Now we watch as a machine with a huge hedge-shearing head on a moveable arm trims an evergreen hedge bordering a distant paddock. In no other place have I seen such meticulously delineated and protected pastures.

We amble past tidy farm yards and lifestyle blocks (one- to ten-acre lots) with extensive beds of shrubs, trees, and other perennial plants. The houses at their centres are modern brick or cement structures, most single-storied, some with jutting or angular facets, and all with metal or clay tile roofs. The contrast between this rural landscape and our own in Nova Scotia is striking. We live in a wood post-and-beam house built a century and a half ago, located in the midst of acres of abandoned farm fields fast reverting to forest; thus, my sons and I are intrigued.

JĀNIS AND DAINIS IN WEST MELTON

Sheepie, tethered off Johnson Road, tolerates our pettings. Farther on, we notice a tiny vineyard, and later a pasture enclosing a red deer herd. We add the deer to our list of livestock thus far observed in Canterbury, a list that includes dairy and beef herds, a surprising number of horses (we learned from Andrea that harness racing is very popular in New Zealand), geese, and many sheep. We spot two burly rams in a paddock; otherwise, ewes fill the pastures. Some are heavy-bellied with pregnancy. Others have young lambs afoot, a sure sign that the southern spring is on its way.

A flurry of movement in a thick hedgerow of trees and

shrubs captures our attention. It's a bird: small, flitting, curious.

"What's that?" Jānis asks excitedly.

I study the bird's field marks. Brown back. Grey head. White eyebrow. Long tail spread in an elegant white-bordered, black-centered fan. "I don't know. I'll look it up in Andrea's bird book when we get back."

Dainis chuckles. "It sure isn't very shy."

The bird flutters around us and perches on the top rail of a wood fence, again fanning its lovely tail.

"I bet that's a *real* New Zealand bird," Jānis states firmly, and Dainis and I agree.

After only two days in New Zealand, we've become well aware of the fact that this country is overrun by introduced species, not just mammals such as the stoats Vilis will be researching, but birds and plants as well. When I saw my first bird here the day we arrived (a European starling) I grumbled, 'Are they everywhere in the world?' On hearing my first bird (a house sparrow) my reaction was the same. Both species were introduced to New Zealand by English colonists seeking to bring a touch of home with them to a new country, as well as to control insect explosions caused by the clearing of native forests to create farmland. [9] So far, the number of introduced bird species we've seen is leading the number of native species five to three. Yet now we have this new bird that we're certain must be a real New Zealand bird, so the ratio is sliding closer to one of equality.

"Look at these *huge* pine cones!" Dainis tugs several heavy cones from sheared pine branches along the roadside. Jānis does the same. The two of them toss the cones high into the air and catch them. They also swing pine branches at a yellow-blossoming, prickly shrub growing along fences. It isn't Scotch broom, as I guessed on our first walk. I had a vague recollection of the time Vilis and I lived in Victoria, British Columbia, where Scotch broom has escaped yards and invaded natural spaces. When I later asked Andrea if I was correct, she replied, 'No, that's gorse. There is some broom around, but it doesn't have thorns.'

Gorse and Scotch broom were brought here by English settlers and have gone wildly astray in this country.[10] Yesterday, while driving in the Port Hills, we saw entire hillsides covered with gorse. With its dense growth and sharp, inch-long thorns, the shrub appeared impenetrable and uneatable. Now, Dainis and Jānis gleefully hack at it with their pine branches as though beheading hostile invaders.

While the boys swing their branches, I spot two spur-winged plovers (brown and white shorebirds) cackling in a roadside pasture. The friendly local couple my sons and I met on our first stroll two days ago asked if we'd seen the plovers yet.

'Are they the noisy birds we see in the pastures?' I asked in return.

'Yeah,' the woman replied, 'but you don't want to get too close. They've got spurs on their wings. I went close to see if there were eggs, and one flew at me.'

The plovers I see now share a pasture with another native shorebird Andrea mentioned I should look for, a heavy-bodied pied (black and white) oystercatcher with a long orange bill. With a name like "oystercatcher," I'm surprised to see the shorebird in a cattle pasture. I tug a notebook from my jacket pocket and jot down the sighting, delighted to be able to add another species to my life list of birds.

On the next leg of our walk, I receive a double avian thrill when I spot an Australian magpie mobbing an Australasian harrier –

a slim brown open-country hawk that's the largest of New Zealand's two native predatory birds. The ratio of introduced to native bird species has suddenly jumped to six apiece, and my initial birding disappointment begins to fade. *Come on, New Zealand! You can do it!*

THE KIDS and I have a lot of time on our hands while staying at Andrea and Andy's home. We can only do so much walking or reading aloud of J. K. Rowling's *Harry Potter and the Goblet of Fire.* On their own, Dainis and Jānis can occupy themselves for only so long by tossing a ball in the yard or playing cards. The books we brought from home are long finished, and they have no toys except a yellow happy-face foam ball Vilis bought for them in Toronto. To alleviate our restlessness while Vilis settles into his work at Landcare, I open a box of school books we brought with us from Canada, and we begin our homeschooling year, three weeks earlier than our usual September start. In contrast to our northern academic schedule, the New Zealand school year is in full swing and will finish with a six-week summer break starting in mid-December.

Seven years ago, when Dainis was old enough to attend kindergarden (called Primary in Nova Scotia) Vilis and I decided to keep him home for the year and teach him his ABCs and numbers ourselves. We gave him simple math booklets, sang songs, played games, took him and Jānis on many walks to look at the world around us, and devoted hours a day to reading aloud to our sons. We had so much fun, we decided to continue year after year. Homeschooling hasn't been a bed of roses, but Dainis and Jānis have retained the wonderful curiosity they showed as toddlers, a curiosity strengthened through their love of reading and scientific experimentation.

Now, they work contentedly to complete math, language arts,

literature, science, and health exercises. They begin to write a "New Zealish"-Canadian dictionary. Already, they've accumulated terms to translate: roundabout = rotary or traffic circle; tomato sauce = ketchup; judder bars = speed bumps; station = ranch; loo = toilet; tramp = hike; brilliant! = great!; and good as gold = okay or goodbye.

Along with interpreting new terms, we're all adjusting to the New Zealand accent speaking familiar words. The vowels seem to be shuffled around, which is no doubt what a Kiwi would say if tossed into a stew pot of Canadian accents. Andrea and Andy are patient with our questions at breakfast and in the evenings after they return from work. They repeat phrases we don't catch and explain unusual terms, traffic rules, and idiosyncrasies of the New Zealand lifestyle. Last evening, I asked about unfamiliar words printed in large letters at the airport in Auckland.

'I saw the words K-I-A O-R-A at the airport. Is it a Māori greeting or welcome?'

'Hey, that's not bad, the way you said "Māori," ' Andrea replied. 'Yeah, it's a greeting, but you say it faster, with the sounds all kind of running together.' She demonstrated, and to me it sounded like a single musically flowing sound: *keeora*.

I mentioned the abundant Māori place names on a map she'd sent Vilis while we were still in Canada and cited a couple I remembered. 'There's a town or city on the North Island and a river with the same name, except that the river starts with *wh* instead of *w*. The city is Wanganui and the river is Whanganui. Was that just a typo?'

'*Ah*,' she responded knowingly. 'In Māori, the letters *wh* are pronounced with a hard *f* sound, so the river is Whanganui.' She pronounced it *Funganooee*. Instantly, my mental image of New Zealand place names took on a new twist.

We're incredibly fortunate to be staying with Andrea and Andy, since both spent four summers at the Arctic Institute of North America's Kluane Lake Research Station in Canada's Yukon Territory. Vilis and I lived there for three years, and Dainis spent his first two years there. Thus, we share many links with the territory, and researchers and base personnel we met there. Our hosts are also nature enthusiasts with a wealth of natural history reference books. Before departing for a long weekend in Otago, the province south of Canterbury, Andrea brings me a stack of field guides. "Thought you might want to have a look through these."

"I'd love to! Thanks." I accept the pile of tree, shrub, bird, and mammal identification guides she thoughtfully hands me, and eagerly flip through the bird guide. In it, I find the lovely little bird the boys and I observed this morning. It's appropriately called a fantail and is very much a New Zealand bird.

August 12

AT 7:15 A.M., Jānis is on the ice in Christchurch, guest skating while Vilis and I scout the coaching staff at the Alpine Ice Sports Centre. The rink is gorgeous, its walls tastefully painted with mountain scenes. It's well lit and much warmer than we're accustomed to in Nova Scotia. A spacious warm room called Zamboni's has a canteen and bar and is located adjacent to the ice surface. A club brochure states that the Centaurus Ice Skating Club has eighty members and offers KiwiSkate (the New Zealand equivalent of Canada's flagship learn-to-skate program, CanSkate) as well as lessons for competitive skaters and adults. Its coaching staff includes two Canadians, an American, and several Kiwis. When Jānis executes a flying camel, he draws interested glances. I later heard that a coach who saw him perform that element knew immediately he was from "the outside."

As peculiar as it may seem, the Alpine Ice Sports Centre's presence near Lincoln was a factor in favour of our choice to spend Vilis's leave in New Zealand. When casting about the globe for possibilities, my husband came up with three potential sites to do his research: Bocas del Toro in Panama, Townsville in northern Australia, and Lincoln. The first two failed in the funding department and the rink department (although Townsville apparently has a half-size rink). Lincoln offered both, giving us the peace of mind that we wouldn't arrive home broke and that Jānis wouldn't be too rusty on his blades when he returns to Nova Scotia.

IN EARLY afternoon, we inspect a brick bungalow in Tai Tapu, a small village six kilometres east of Lincoln near the base of the Port Hills. The pros are that the house is located beside a primary school, is graced by a magnolia in the front yard, is inexpensive to rent, and is within easy driving or cycling distance from Vilis's workplace in Lincoln. The cons are that it's plain and drab. Having previously agreed that our dollars in New Zealand are earmarked for adventure, Vilis and I decide the house will do for our stay in the country. Charles, our prospective landlord, bubbles with enthusiasm beneath a mop of black curls. He's keen to rent, and we agree to move in the following weekend after some repairs are completed.

Buoyed by our success at finding a house so quickly and longing to stretch our legs on a hike, we drive southeast from Tai Tapu into brown hills that rise to Lyttelton Volcano's crater rim. Near Gebbies Pass, we locate the trailhead for Mount Bradley Walkway.

AT THE TRAILHEAD OF MOUNT BRADLEY WALKWAY

New Zealand has hundreds of tracks, many of which are available to the public even though they pass through privately owned land (as does Mount Bradley Walkway). In this country, hiking or "tramping" is a national hobby.

Viewed from the trailhead, the Port Hills on the far side of Lyttelton Harbour appear rumpled and dented by narrow valleys, with the harbour a pale blue sheet at their feet. Closer to hand, sheep droppings litter cropped grasses and herbs growing between tussocks that form greenish-gold fans taller than my knees. Ewes and a few lambs graze in rolling pastures below the pass. Two Australasian harriers cruise on V-wings above the pastures as we begin our hike.

"What does that sign say?" I ask, looking ahead to a white board nailed to a fence post. Too soon we read the discouraging words: TRACK CLOSED DUE TO LAMBING.

Still keen to hike, we drive north on Summit Road to Ōmahu Bush near Cooper's Knob, a rounded outcrop on the crater rim that resembles a weathered brow with a peculiar growth attached to it. The "bush," we discover, is an almost impenetrable jungle of thin, stunted trees (all unknown to us). Some are twisted and tangled with vines. Streamers of orange bark peel from the trunks of others (native fuchsias, I later learned).

"These are weird woods," Dainis comments. Always a climber, he scales tree after tree. Fantails flutter around him and fly among us, their tails spread in elegant, charming displays as the tiny birds hunt insects disturbed by our movements.

The track leads from "weird woods" hugging the road's edge onto open grassland where we link up with a gentle grassland trail called Prendergast's Track. After we hike a short distance, Vilis gestures to the upswept profile of a small volcanic cone to the west and suggests, "Let's climb that instead."

We abandon the track and scale the tussock-tufted base of Gibraltar Rock, then its rocky upper reaches. The boys laugh with excitement, and Dainis, who'd been torn to leave his Canadian home, exclaims, "I didn't know we would be climbing mountains!"

From the summit, the view stretches as wide as our hearts, west across the Canterbury Plain's farmland to the Southern Alps and north to Christchurch's streets and the ocean. Here, atop this classic volcanic cone, our New Zealand outdoor adventures begin.

CANTERBURY PLAIN AND DISTANT SOUTHERN ALPS SEEN FROM
GIBRALTAR ROCK

August 13

THIS SUNDAY morning, frost is a veil of diamonds on West Melton roadsides as I run for the first time on New Zealand soil. Later, I drive the rural community's quiet roads to familiarize myself with the Blue Bomb. The station wagon's gears are tough, and before I turned the ignition key, I reached again and again for the seatbelt on my left, until light broke through in my North American mind. *Drive on the left. Steering wheel and seatbelt on the right.* This is another legacy of British colonization of New Zealand.

I'M THE excursion planner in our family. Already, I've earmarked pages and highlighted sentences and paragraphs in our New Zealand travel guide. So far, I've focused on the Christchurch area and have plans for us to tramp scenic Crater Rim Walkway in the Port Hills, explore Banks Peninsula with its pastures and many tracks, and hunt for jade on the beach at Birdlings Flat. The possibilities seem endless, but those will do for a start.

In early afternoon, we head for Kennedy's Bush Track on the slopes of the Port Hills. Vilis takes a wrong turn, and we end up in a picnic park located on what was formerly the base of Halswell Quarry. Intrigued by a rock amphitheatre that curves around a lush lawn, we stroll across the vivid grass and learn from interpretive displays that the quarry site was once a small volcanic cone. Here, black basalt was cut from the extinct volcano for more than a century until 1990, when the rock gave out and the quarry closed. This quarry, which once yielded building stone for the steps, walls, and pavings of much of Christchurch's architecture, now offers the city's residents green space for relaxation and play, an excellent example of ecological restoration.[11]

After we leave the quarry, we successfully locate Kennedy's

Bush Road and drive to the trailhead for Kennedy's Bush Track. From the car park, a vista of hills, plain, and mountains entices us, however, we're again halted by a "TRACK CLOSED DUE TO LAMBING" sign. According to the sign, sheep will rule Canterbury's hiking trails for six more weeks.

"Aw!" Jānis groans.

"*Six weeks!*" I grumble, and Vilis and Dainis also voice their disappointment.

I know it's reasonable that pastoralists (sheep or cattle farmers) would want to minimize stresses to ewes during lambing, yet my family chafes at the restriction. Six weeks is an eighth of our time in this country. To be blocked again and again from exploring Canterbury's beckoning landscapes is like seeing ice cream in a cage and not being able to reach through the bars to get to it. But we'll keep reaching.

August 14

AGAIN, FROST sparkles on the ground as I run a five-kilometre loop of West Melton roads in face-biting, early morning cold. Mallards gabble. Spur-winged plovers cackle and screech their defensive calls. Silver plumes of breath puff from my mouth, and I hear too many birds I cannot see and do not know. For a confessed birder, this is a mild form of torture.

A LIBRARY is a gift, a wondrous gift. As soon as Lincoln Public Library opens, we enter its book-filled space. Now that we have an address at which we'll be living in Tai Tapu, we're able to get library cards. We load up with books...books for fun, books for interest, and many, many books about New Zealand.

When we're finished at the library, Vilis drives the boys and me back to Andrea and Andy's home before leaving for work. His current life is a stir-fry of domestic and research responsibilities. He can't abandon us to our own devices during the day because I have no means of transportation in West Melton, yet he must pursue his stoat research. Today, my sons' and my gift is the library. Today and for the next ten months, Vilis's gift is being surrounded by ecologists conducting wildlife research.

AFTER LUNCH, my kids and I walk a new loop of country roads, an outing that stretches into two-and-a-half hours of exercise and observation. We spot a grey warbler, a native species, in a pine hedge. Its white tail tips are conspicuous, and its song is a rich musical trill. House sparrows and rock pigeons feed in and around a horse trough, and greenfinches and European goldfinches, all introduced species, bob up and down as they feed in a pasture. Once again, the avian equation tilts in favour of introduced species.

WITH DARKNESS falling early, evenings stretch long in a home that isn't our own. As exciting as it is to be living in a foreign country, we already miss the familiarity of our Canadian home, Ravenhill. A renovated old farmhouse, its large windows look onto meadows, forests, and my flowerbeds and fruit and vegetable gardens. The boys are accustomed to cycling, playing sports in our large yard, and helping to care for chickens and pet cats (when we left, we gave the poultry away, and our tenant promised to look after the cats). Our sons also enjoyed board games and LEGO with friends, and playing our piano. They can do none of those things here at Andrea and Andy's home.

Tonight, Dainis curls up like a cat in front of the log burner (wood stove) in a nook between the kitchen and dining room. Vilis, Jānis, and I read on huge, plump cushions in the dining room or on the small couch near the log burner. When restlessness sets in, Vilis invents a game for us to play. He hides the boys' small yellow happy-face foam ball in such a way that it's visible from the couch, but is in an unlikely place. Whoever spots it has the privilege of hiding it next. Excitement and laughter fill the house as we spot the ball tucked between two couch cushions, on top of the fridge in the kitchen, on a window sill, tucked among the pieces of wood for the log burner, or among the clothes in a laundry hamper.

Before bedtime, Vilis writes a note for Andrea and Andy, who have not yet returned from Alexandra, telling them that we (not burglars) will be up and about in their house in the dark of early morning.

August 15

AT 6:00 A.M., the Alpine Ice Sports Centre's attractiveness is diminished by the cold within its mountain-painted walls. It may be warmer than Nova Scotia rinks; nonetheless it's a rink, and Canterbury is still in the throes of winter. While Jānis skates for two hours, I observe coaches. Beside me, Vilis and Dainis read and shiver.

Back in West Melton, we devour a hot porridge breakfast, then Vilis leaves for work. I begin reading aloud to the boys from Peggy Dunstan's *A Fistful of Summer*, a book of recollections about growing up in Christchurch and Wellington. In the first chapter we meet four-year-old Peggy, who's thrilled to ride a train decorated with banners and smoked saveloys, from Lyttelton to Christchurch and then south to Motukarara to attend a pork butchers' picnic.

"What's a saveloy?" both Dainis and Jānis ask, stumbling

over the unfamiliar word.

"I don't know," I answer. "I'm not even sure how to pronounce it. Is it 'SAVE-loy' or 'SAV-eloy'? *Hmm.* Let's keep reading."

Peggy attends the picnic and is enchanted by jammy buns, tables of sweets, tiny spigots on beer kegs, and a seven- or eight-year-old boy who wins the bun-eating contest by chewing a bun off a string, and then consuming it and a mouthful of dirt while crouched on the ground. We wait for more information about those saveloys, but the term isn't mentioned again.[12] (Later, I asked a butcher in Lincoln about saveloys. He pronounced the word "SAV-eloys" and showed me bright red sausages in his display case.)

After schoolwork is completed and lunch consumed, I tuck my small notebook into my jacket pocket, and the boys and I stroll neighbourhood roads. I point out male and female blackbirds, a pair of mallards, a fantail and a magpie, as well as a mixed flock of goldfinches, redpolls, and skylarks feeding in a pasture. I record each sighting in my notebook and add other notes about West Melton. While we're based at Andrea and Andy's home, with hours of free time and few domestic responsibilities, the frequent opportunities to go birding are as much a blessing as an indulgence.

Before supper, (called "tea" here: more fodder for the "New Zealish"-Canadian dictionary) I relate my bird sightings to Andy and summarize by saying, "I've seen eighteen species so far, and twelve are new for me!"

He smiles knowingly. "Ah, you're a twitcher."

A twitcher is a compulsive birder obsessed with adding rare species to his or her life list. I'm keen, but I'd never drop everything and fly across a country to look at a bird. I shake my head. "No, I'm not a twitcher, but I do like to keep records."

At home in Nova Scotia, I have a stack of coil-bound exercise books filled with natural history observations that date back to the late seventies. They document plant and wildlife species and landscapes I've seen. I've discovered that the act of identifying a bird or frog or tree, whether easy or difficult, catapults my awareness of the world around me into a new realm filled with fascinating connections. By identifying and observing another organism, I myself feel more closely linked with this planet we all call home. Many of my observations have made their way into freelance articles I've written about wildlife for the children's nature magazine *Ranger Rick*.

August 16

AFTER VILIS returns from Landcare to spend the afternoon with us, I run West Melton roadsides and discover that carnage on the highway is as prevalent in New Zealand as it is in Canada. However, rather than encountering road-killed porcupines, skunks, and raccoons – native mammals I encounter on my runs in Canada – I run past a squashed stoat and hedgehog, both introduced mammals here in New Zealand.

Seeing the stoat and hedgehog makes me think about this country's history. New Zealand was the last large, inhabitable land mass to be populated by humans.[13] The first arrivals, Polynesian explorers, came ashore around a thousand years ago and took up residence at about the same time the Byzantine civilization entered its last golden age and Leif Eriksson explored North America's northeast coast to discover Newfoundland for Europeans. Unfortunately, the Polynesian explorers, and later, European explorers and settlers, opened an ecological Pandora's box of introduced weeds and pests and spilled its contents onto these southern islands. Those weeds and pests have created something of a nightmare.

INVASIVE SPECIES

"Hindsight is 20/20," as the saying goes. It certainly applies to invasive species in New Zealand. In their native countries, species introduced to New Zealand (stoat and hedgehog, for example) face natural checks and balances. However, in New Zealand they and other introduced species don't face the same checks and balances as in their native countries. As a result, their populations have exploded and their ranges have expanded, causing far-reaching, disastrous effects on New Zealand ecosystems. (For example, stoats prey heavily on New Zealand birds. Hedgehogs eat New Zealand invertebrates and lizards, as well as birds' eggs and young.[14]) The unforeseen consequences of introducing non-native species to New Zealand have created this country's biggest ecological challenge: controlling invasive species.

On my return to Andrea and Andy's house, I mention the road-killed stoat, the first stoat I've seen since our arrival.

"So, they're right here," Vilis muses. He eyes me quizzically. "Do you know something? At Landcare, I was asked what the top priority is for wildlife biologists in Canada. I said, 'Habitat management.' Do you know what the top priority is for wildlife biologists in New Zealand? Killing mammals. In Canada, my research is *studying* mammals, and here they're doing everything they can to kill them."

To the uninitiated, Vilis's comments may sound extreme and overly critical, yet they highlight an important distinction between the basic ecologies of many other countries and that of New Zealand. In Canada, for example, land mammals of various sizes and lifestyles (such as deer mice, wolves, and moose) are an integral part of the native fauna (animal life). However, the same is not true in New Zealand.

Before humans arrived on these islands, the only mammals present were three species of bats (thought to have flown to the islands), two of which have survived to the present.[15] *There were no other mammals.* This is a huge ecological difference and one that New Zealand's settlers saw as a liability they needed to overcome. With the exception of the native bats, all wild mammals currently existing in this country are the descendants of mammals introduced by explorers and colonists.

Many introduced mammals have spread throughout the country and are destructive pests. However, some pests, like deer and wild pigs, are valued by hunters as sport animals. Thus, conservation agencies such as Landcare Research and the Department of Conservation are faced with the conundrum of deciding how to balance the interests of sport hunters with the desire to preserve native ecosystems and protect threatened species from the ravages inflicted by introduced species, the most destructive of which are mammals.[16] Time will tell where their decisions lead.

LATER IN the afternoon, I drive Jānis to the rink. He's finding his skating legs again and looks stronger than he did during his first two skates. Although we've dealt with some necessities for establishing our lives here, such as locating a house to rent, opening a bank account, obtaining library cards, and arranging for Dainis and Jānis to attend Scout and Cub meetings next week, other aspects of our existence remain up in the air: finding a coach for Jānis, inquiring about tennis lessons for Dainis, and settling into our own space. Thankfully, we'll be able to move into the Tai Tapu bungalow on the weekend. As wonderfully generous as Andrea and Andy have been, my family needs space of our own.

August 17

AT THE rink, unknown faces glide past me. My new skates cramp and chafe. I move cautiously, terrified of falling. It's ironic that a Canadian should learn to skate properly in a country other than her own, but here I am at the Alpine Ice Sports Centre, which I've learned is one of only nine rinks in New Zealand. Six of these rinks, including two outdoor rinks, are spread across the southern half of South Island. Two of the three remaining rinks are located in Auckland, and the last is here in Christchurch.

"You want to have both feet on the ice as little as possible," Chris Street tells me. He's a twenty-something, red-haired, national ice dance champion and instructor for the Thursday morning Coffee Club adult group lesson.

"Okay," I say and begin the perilous journey toward gliding on one blade at a time. When my toe picks catch the ice, I thud painfully to my knees. At the end of the one-hour lesson, my feet are screaming. *What am I doing here?* Maybe my decision to learn to skate as a break from the constant demands of caring for and teaching my children wasn't the wisest.

On my return to West Melton, Vilis leaves for Landcare, and my sons and I dive into New Zealand history. We learn that these islands split away from the ancient supercontinent of Gondwanaland long before that gigantic landmass broke apart to form Australia, India, Africa, South America, and Antarctica.[17]

Isolated for eons of time and by thousands of kilometres of ocean, the islands that now form New Zealand developed a unique flora resplendent with ancient fern-rich forests, with 80 percent of their species found nowhere else on earth.[18] The islands also developed a fauna that lacked mammals. There were no mice or rats. Instead, large insects filled those ecological roles. There were no deer or sheep. Instead, large flightless birds such as geese, rails, and in particular, about a dozen moa species, filled the roles of major herbivores, grazing or browsing plants. The moa (all extinct now) ranged from chicken-size to three metres tall and weighed up to 250 kilograms.

THE HUMAN FACTOR

With the arrival of humans came predation and habitat loss not previously experienced by New Zealand's native bird populations. The Polynesian explorers and their descendants hunted all the moa species to extinction, including giant moa (the largest bird ever known). They burned large forest tracts to create gardens and introduced rats and dogs, which are very effective nest predators. The Māori had exterminated nearly forty bird species (almost half the number of species nesting on the main islands) before Europeans set foot on this land in the late 1700s.[19]

European explorers were followed by sealers, whalers, traders, and settlers who brought songbirds, livestock, other rats and house mice, hedgehogs, game animals such as rabbits and deer, and brushtail possums. All these mammals competed with native birds for food and space, which also affected native flora. Introduced plants such as gorse and Scotch broom competed with native plants, disrupting native food webs. Timber was harvested for shipbuilding and export and burned to clear land for agriculture, destroying vast areas of native forest and, thus, bird habitat.[20]

In the late 1800s, the introduced rabbit population exploded. Three mustelids (mammals of the weasel family, distinguished by a long body, short legs, and musky scent glands under the tail) – weasels, stoats, and ferrets – were introduced to control the pests. This was perhaps the final blow to native bird species and one from which they haven't recovered. It soon became obvious that weasels, stoats, and ferrets don't just hunt rabbits; they also hunt birds. Stoats have been classified as public enemy number one of New Zealand birds and are the brown kiwi's arch enemy, credited with killing a heartbreaking 95 percent of the young kiwi hatched.[21]

The Department of Conservation has eliminated rats from several offshore islands, returning them to predator-free status.[22] It has also funded studies aimed at eliminating mustelids from certain locales. One of these studies is Vilis's research, to determine how far juvenile stoats disperse in order to calculate how large an area must be trapped free of stoats to be kept stoat-free.

Until Polynesian seafarers discovered these islands, New

Zealand was a land dominated by birds.[23] Some, like the extinct moa and today's extant kiwi, were or are flightless. Many others, flightless or not, nested or nest on the ground, making them vulnerable to predation.

For so long, these islands lay alone in the southern ocean, unknown and unspoiled by mankind, a land of birds. "I wish I could have seen it," I tell Dainis and Jānis, my birder's heart yearning.

"Yeah," Jānis agrees. "I wish I could have seen the moas."

Dainis nods. "Yeah. The moas."

Unfortunately, the moa are no more, and many of New Zealand's remaining native birds are fighting for their lives.

August 19

FOR THE second day in a row, branches flail in a wild wind and cold rain pours from the sky. I catch a snippet of radio news informing the public that highways north and south of Christchurch are closed due to flooding. The names of the rivers causing this emergency are fleeting wisps of sound to a newcomer like me. The rivers themselves are apparently swollen torrents fed by mountain run-off, rushing in essentially straight lines from the Southern Alps to the Pacific.

Dainis and I hole up at Andrea's and Andy's house while Vilis and Jānis attend a police general auction in Christchurch during the stormy afternoon. Yesterday, the four of us attended a police bicycle auction, where Vilis bid for, and won, nine bicycles. Three of them are junk, but he plans to salvage enough parts to create four fully functional bicycles so we can cycle as a family, and the boys and I can explore farther afield while he's at work. Today, he and Jānis return from the general auction with our station wagon full of camping equipment, outdoor clothing, and supplies for the home we thought we'd rented.

I say "thought we'd rented" because last evening when Vilis rang Charles of the black curls to confirm our move to Tai Tapu, he received the unapologetic news that our landlord had sold the bungalow two days after we viewed it. 'He didn't even have the decency to tell us,' Vilis said, his hand slicing sharp, frustrated gestures in the air. 'We wasted all that time when we could have been looking.' Our opinion of that New Zealander took a nosedive. Andrea looked on anxiously, empathizing with our disappointment.

This evening, we battle that disappointment and storm woes by playing "five hundred" (a card game similar to bridge) with our hosts. Dainis and Jānis are fast becoming card sharks, aided and abetted by Andrea, who has shown a heart-warming interest in the boys. Seated across from me, Andy is pokerfaced and appears impervious to the cold to which my family is not yet accustomed. He wears red shorts, puffy insulated booties, and a Toronto Maple Leafs jersey. Andrea, dressed in jeans and a light V-neck sweater, offers occasional clarifying bits of advice on the game. Hardy Canadians that we are, Vilis, the boys, and I sit bundled in sweatshirts and sweaters and play hand after hand while the winter storm wails beyond the walls.

"Would you like a hottie?" Andy asks, having noticed my shivering after the game. He indicates a hot water bottle on the counter.

"Oh, yes!"

He flips the switch on a 220-volt electric kettle, which boils up water much faster than my 110-volt kettle in Canada. He fills the hot water bottle and hands it to me. I snuggle thankfully into bed with its heat pressed tightly against me. *When will this New Zealand winter end?*

August 21

AGAIN TODAY, cold rain grips Canterbury in its fist. Dainis and Jānis light a fire in the log burner at Andrea and Andy's house and complete their schoolwork crouched at a coffee table in front of the flames. When a break in the rain occurs, the three of us abandon the house for a ride on our bicycles. We glory in the swift passage of pavement beneath our tires as we zip past sodden green pastures walled by soaring, straight-sided hedges that bar entry to the wind and all else.

When we resume schooling, I read to the boys the legend of Māui, who was a great Māori hero of creation's early days when men and gods were alike. Māui sailed far south from his homeland of Hawaiki with his brothers. When their food supplies dwindled, he hit his nose with his grandmother's jawbone, causing his blood to spill upon the bone. Then he cast into the great waters this hook and snagged a gargantuan fish. The ocean giant battled Māui until he yanked it from the depths to form North Island, Te Ika-a-Māui, "The Fish of Māui."[24] This legend is our first taste of Māori culture.

Historians believe New Zealand's first people arrived from East Polynesia in ocean-going canoes a thousand or more years ago. Perhaps they came from Tahiti or the Cook Islands or the Marquesas Islands. Perhaps they were blown off course in storms. They may have left hunger and poor living conditions behind, been driven away by enemies, or were explorers intent on seeking out new lands. No one knows for sure. At least some of the arrivals brought dogs and rats, as well as yams, *taro*, and tubers of *kūmara* (sweet potato), indicating that they had planned a long journey.[25]

And it certainly was a long journey. The islands they paddled from lie more than 3 000 kilometres away from this country's main islands, across open ocean. New Zealand's nearest neighbour is

Australia, more than 2 000 kilometres away. It's safe to say that this country is a long way from anywhere. Yet, those Polynesian adventurers, ancestors of the Māori, found this land and were the first humans to walk on it. They named it Aotearoa (usually translated as "Land of the Long White Cloud," but also as "Land of the Long Daylight")[26] and it became their home.

WE'VE FOUND a potential house to rent! Yesterday, sunshine chased away cloud and soothed the earth, assuring us the weekend storm had passed. Again, we studied houses to let (for rent) in the Lincoln and Tai Tapu areas and eventually eliminated all but one Andrea had mentioned to us, an older clapboard bungalow owned by Crop & Food Research on North Belt in Lincoln.

Painted beige with brown trim, the bungalow is almost next door to Lincoln Domain (recreation park) which has a Scout Hall, tennis courts, and rugby field. Yesterday, from an arched opening in the hedge fronting the yard, I noticed ornamental shrubs on a spacious lawn bordered by hedges and walls. I saw weeds cluttering a small garden patch on the north side of the house. Gardener that I am, they made my fingers itch to pull them out.

The house has large panel windows overlooking its yard, which is surprisingly and attractively secluded. I loved the spacious feel of the property, as did Vilis, Dainis, and Jānis. Plenty of room for romping there. After a quick look at the house and yard, we checked out Lincoln, which is known as a "township" rather than a town. (Lincoln was established as Lincoln Village in 1863, thirteen years after Canterbury's first settlers arrived from England.[27])

Commercial buildings and government offices, including Landcare Research, line Lincoln's main drag, Gerald Street. Two dozen residential streets flank Gerald Street. These streets feature neat, primarily single-story houses, almost all of which possess walled yards every bit as manicured as West Melton's yards. A greenbelt called Liffey Reserve borders a creek, and Lincoln University's residence towers and elegant brick buildings rise above surrounding farmland.

'It's basically a government and university town,' Vilis explained yesterday as we drove Lincoln's streets. 'Around two thousand people live here, but the population jumps when school's in at Lincoln University. A lot of government workers commute here, too.'

'We could walk almost everywhere,' I commented, thinking that the boys and I would enjoy exploring Liffey Reserve and the shops on foot. And Vilis could easily walk or cycle to work. My spirits lifted. Perhaps the Tai Tapu house debacle was a blessing in disguise.

August 22

AT 6:30 P.M., Lincoln Scout Hall's cement block walls loom tall and wide around Jānis. His tan-coloured, button-up Canadian Cub shirt differs conspicuously from the dark green jerseys (pullovers) worn by the Lincoln Cubs. Shy and self-conscious, Jānis chews his lip while the local Cubs zoom around him. They point at badges on his red over-the-shoulder sash, and ask him questions in accents he has difficulty understanding.

Lincoln Koreke Cub Pack leader or "Akela," Andrew Wallace, is a slim, energetic, grey-haired man. He calls the Pack to order and introduces Jānis. My son is soon caught up in a minefield game and then listens attentively while three Cubs present independent projects called Kiwi Projects. Vilis, Dainis, and I observe the meeting from a bench at the end of the hall so Jānis won't feel alone. At the hour's end, my nine-year-old is again the centre of attention. When we exit the hall, he radiates excitement and relief.

After Dainis and Jānis are in bed, I telephone Kim Lewis, one of the Canadian skating coaches at the Alpine Ice Sports Centre, and ask her to coach Jānis. To my relief, she agrees. Along with a spiked hairdo and megawatt smile, Kim has first-rate qualifications, but more important, she speaks English with an accent Jānis can understand.

With Kim's agreement, a loose peg in our lives finds a hole. Another loose peg still rattling around is arranging Dainis's tennis lessons, which will begin in October. Today, however, we popped the largest loose peg into a hole when we arranged to rent the clapboard bungalow in Lincoln.

This morning, we inspected the interior of the house. It appeared dismal at first glance, with a stained carpet, torn wallpaper in the hallway, and a beige kitchen made even more dreary by dark brown cupboards. However, further inspection revealed plenty of large windows, an airy living room, a welcoming master bedroom, a smaller second bedroom, and a room I can use as a study. A huge bonus is the secluded, spacious yard graced by lilacs, a large shade tree, shrub fuchsias, hydrangeas, and a lemon tree growing beside the back door. Nonetheless, our rental agreement hinges on a guarantee of carpet cleaning, new paint for the kitchen, and repairs to the hallway walls. Even though we'll be in New Zealand less than a year, we need this house to be our sanctuary. We want to enjoy it.

August 24

YESTERDAY, ENERGY sizzled within us as we prepared to leave West Melton. The time until noon stretched too long, so the boys and I filled it with running, reading, cycling, cleaning, and packing. Then Vilis and the station wagon appeared, and we left Andrea and Andy's home, so thankful for our hosts' generosity, yet keen to settle into our own place.

In Lincoln, Dainis and Jānis cycled around and around the clapboard bungalow on North Belt, grinning with excitement. Vilis and I opened every window to let in some fresh air. Then, with the thrill of anticipation, we unpacked from the car the bits and pieces of the lives we'll make in Lincoln. As a last task, we laid sleeping bags on the bedroom floors in readiness for our first night in our new home.

THIS MORNING, frost lies like the kiss of death on grass and trees in the yard. Inside the bungalow, our breaths puff from our mouths in silvery clouds. All night, bitter cold attacked us while we attempted to sleep on the floor of this empty house with open crawl space beneath it. Now, we cluster, shivering, in the kitchen, around two electric heaters Vilis bought yesterday. Our bodies ache from a night on the floor. Dainis's lips are blue. He presses his arms tightly against his sides and blurts, "I think I know why we've seen so few fat New Zealanders."

The rest of us exclaim, "Because they use all their energy trying to stay warm!"

"I was all right as long as I huddled up," Jānis qualifies.

A cold meal of Hubbards Fruitful Breakfast and milk, eaten standing up or seated on the floor, serves as another chilling welcome. However, by late morning, sunshine has erased the frost. It warms the boys and me when we cycle out of Lincoln past a hospital, golf course, and farm fields.

LATE IN the afternoon, the delicious warmth is gone. Darkness envelopes the car in which Dainis and I ride to the shooting range in Tai Tapu, the village at the base of the Port Hills. At the range, the Lincoln Scouts and their moms will blast away at targets with .22 calibre rifles in a shoot-off. Such will be Dainis's introduction to Scouting in New Zealand. *Fascinating.* Dainis has never been anywhere near a shooting range. Nor have I.

A pot-bellied stove in the gun clubhouse battles cold that sweeps into the room each time a shooter enters or leaves the adjacent shooting gallery. Dainis and I wait our turns, and I notice that although he's shy, he's not as intimidated at being tossed into a group of unknown youths as Jānis. He plays with a puppy and cheerfully enters into games with the other Scouts. They don't swarm around him, like the Cubs did around Jānis. Rather, they approach and depart from him casually, as befitting their teen and pre-teen "coolness."

The wait seems endless, but at last, it's my turn to challenge Dainis. Together, we push through flaps to the unheated shooting gallery. We're instructed how to assume the correct prone position, how to hold the rifle, and how to sight the targets, which are eleven small black circles on a rectangular sheet of paper at the gallery's far end. I have no idea what the shooting distance is and am so cold I can't imagine hitting any of the targets. Yet, when I place ear protectors over my ears and sight my first target I become consumed by the challenge and all else disappears, leaving only the rifle and me.

Dainis scores 52 points. Amazingly, I score 81 points. The moms win. On the return drive to Lincoln, the voices of Sarah and her mother (the Scout-mom pair with whom Dainis and I caught a ride to Tai Tapu) flow over me like bending, flexing fingers that transform the English language I thought I knew into sounds that leap and shush, stretch, and simply fade away.

August 27

TODAY, LATE winter sunshine entices us into the Port Hills. To the east, green mounded hilltops, patched with blooming gorse, roll down to Lyttelton Harbour's pale blue. With no fences to confine them atop the hills, beef cattle bolt across Summit Road.

CATTLE GRAZING IN THE PORT HILLS

Freed from the wildly unsettled weather of the past few days (wind, hail, rain intermixed with sun) we tramp north through pastures on a section of Crater Rim Walkway, a forty-kilometre track that parallels Summit Road. Patches of gorse, broom, and the dense, stunted woods Dainis labelled "weird woods" intermittently edge or engulf the track we share with other trampers, and occasionally with sheep. Cattle stare while the boys laughingly fling themselves from the dirt track onto densely twigged mats of shrubs beaded with pale, unfurling leaves. High above us, an Australasian harrier and a slim man-made glider float above the hills.

We soon abandon the trail to investigate an escarpment that drops from the crater rim to low hills and lush pastures near the harbour. Shallow caves eroded into the rock wall spark our imaginations. We talk of one day camping here, high above two narrow, snaking peninsulas that stretch their arms toward Quail Island in the harbour's centre. From our vantage point, we observe speedboats and a container ship plying the serene harbour water. Closer to hand, a welcome swallow with deep curves of speed in its wings and grace in its long forked tail flashes past the caves' mouths as though claiming possession.

AT AN ESCARPMENT OVERLOOKING LYTTELTON HARBOUR

After we return to the track, we continue northward and cross Summit Road, pausing to explore a rest stop called Sign of the Bellbird. Here, an eco-friendly (composting) toilet, the stone remains of a teahouse, and a sturdy shelter built from rocks salvaged from the teahouse stand amid tall, shading trees.

From the shelter, we gaze to the west at Kennedy's Bush Reserve, an expanse of forested hills sandwiched between the crater rim and the Canterbury Plain's farmland. Elsewhere in these hills, little forest remains. I've learned such was not the case when New

Zealand was a land of birds. Before the arrival of humans, trees covered 80 percent of this country's landscape. Stewart Island was completely forested, as was North Island, except for peaks on the Central Volcanic Plateau and inland water bodies like vast Lake Taupō. South Island was also largely forested, but featured pockets of native scrub, fern, grassland, and alpine vegetation, as well as large lakes and the barren, exposed peaks of the Southern Alps.[28]

After leaving Sign of the Bellbird, we hike Holdsworth Track through a golden sea of tussock grasses. Trees with wildly untidy heads of dagger-like leaves punctuate the grassland.

"Are these palm trees?" Jānis asks.

"I don't think so." I decide to buy field guides to New Zealand vegetation and birds during the coming week.

"Whatever they are, they're fun to climb," Dainis calls from a tree crotch below three spiky heads.

ON HOLDSWORTH TRACK

Haze blurs the agricultural plain far below the golden slope. Cloud rolls in over the hills, hinting at rain. As we hurry back to Sign of the Bellbird and then to the car, spitting rain begins to fall. In Nova Scotia, we have an adage: "If you don't like the weather, wait a minute and it will change." That adage seems to fit Canterbury as well.

GONE ARE the days of living as guests in someone else's fully-equipped home. Since moving to Lincoln four days ago, we've been immersed in a scramble to set up house. Already, we've spent many hours shopping for necessities at crowded malls, a recycling centre, and second-hand furniture stores in Christchurch. The boys have been agog with curiosity during our shopping expeditions, as they have during our hikes and drives on Summit Road, with its superfit cyclists and runners. Like Vilis and me, they're soaking up New Zealand and formulating their own impressions, trying to pinpoint aspects of New Zealand's character. Yesterday, after we threaded our way through large crowds of shoppers in Christchurch malls, Dainis grinned and said, "I have another theory. All the New Zealanders who aren't out exercising are at the shopping malls!"

One of our best shopping finds to date is a huge wooden kitchen table, which we use for homeschooling. At present, the kitchen is the only room we spend any "awake" time in. That's because it has two portable heaters, which we now move into the bedrooms for the night.

Two days after our memorably frigid first night, I strolled to the butcher shop to buy mince (ground beef) for hamburgers. I told the man working at the counter that we'd just moved to Lincoln on Wednesday and that we absolutely froze that night.

'Wednesday?' He smiled at the irony. 'That was probably the coldest night of the winter.'

No wonder we shivered through it.

Along with the newness of settling into the old bungalow, we've experienced our first language faux pas. Vilis returned from Landcare three days ago with words of caution pertaining to "New Zealish." He said, 'You can't call a fanny pack a fanny pack here. Call it a bum bag. At coffee break, I happened to mention my fanny pack, and people were really grossed out. Apparently, "fanny" is a really crude word for a vagina.' The boys and I gaped. I wondered what other vulgarities we'd innocently spoken. Although Canada and New Zealand share English as an official language, some Kiwi words obviously have different connotations than the same words in Canada.

This evening, we hole up in the kitchen and close its two doors against winter cold that stalks us in the rest of the house. Dainis sits on a heater, and we drink steaming cups of tea or milk with Milo (a malt-and-chocolate-flavoured, supposedly nutritious drink powder). Vilis pulls out a deck of cards, and we play spoons, then read novels, battling winter's chill with the warmth of laughter and a thousand images from other places.

August 28

OUR LIFE in Lincoln is slowly taking shape. We've arranged a three-month block of skating lessons for Jānis and have accumulated more New Zealish phrases. We've also bought several pieces of furniture to begin to fill the empty bungalow. The boys now have beds, and today Vilis brings home a desk for me as well as a dresser for our bedroom and one for the boys' room. My sons and I clean the furniture and, like eagles building a stick nest, push and tug the furniture into position.

This country has no eagles now. Its only two native predatory bird species, the New Zealand falcon and Australasian harrier, are much smaller and less imposing than Canadian eagles. In Nova Scotia, I frequently observe bald eagles perched beside or cruising above Waugh River. When Vilis, Dainis, and I lived in Yukon Territory, we watched golden eagles soar over autumn-rich tundra in the Ogilvie Mountains. Yet, those eagles and even the harpy eagle (the world's largest living eagle) pale in comparison with an eagle that once lived in New Zealand.

Named for Julius van Haast, who first directed the Canterbury Museum, the Haast eagle was the tiger of New Zealand. It weighed up to eighteen kilograms and had a wingspan of up to three metres, as well as talons the size of a tiger's claws. In the same way that tigers and lions hunt grazing and browsing mammals, often much larger than they are, the Haast eagle hunted giant, plant-eating birds, notably the giant moa. A hunting Haast eagle launched its massive body from forest perches and slammed into prey at speeds of up to 80 kilometres per hour. After knocking its upcoming meal to the ground, it crushed and ripped the prey's neck and skull with its massive talons.[29]

Pairs of Haast eagles occupied territories encompassing hundreds of square kilometres of forest. No doubt they encountered (perhaps as dinner!) this country's early human inhabitants, who named these birds *pouakai* or *hokio*. After moa became extinct, the giant eagle, like its walking food supply, slid into memory and archaeology.[30] Part of me wishes I could have seen one, but part of me is afraid it would have seen *me* first.

YET AGAIN, cold rain pours down onto Lincoln. It nixes outdoor jaunts for the boys and me and instead burdens us with the task of keeping warm. Dainis occupies himself with designing a form to record details for three outdoor adventures that demonstrate

increasing levels of difficulty. These adventures are required to earn
the Explorer badge in Canadian Scouting. (He's working at earning
both Canadian and New Zealand Scouting badges.) He types onto
our laptop the following headings: *Expedition. Date. Place. Type.
Distance. Other Factors. Risks. Precautions. Evaluation.* Already, he has an
idea for the first expedition: a return twenty-one-kilometre cycling
excursion from Lincoln to Tai Tapu that would include a circuit of
rural roads at the Port Hills' base. Another possibility we discuss is a
campout in the escarpment's shallow caves high above Lyttelton
Harbour, although he exhibits markedly less enthusiasm for this idea.

"I think I'd worry all night about rolling off the edge," he
explains.

And we, unlike the welcome swallow that floated so
effortlessly past the caves' entrances, have no wings to lift us back to
safety.

August 29

OUR TRAVEL to this country caused us to flip from a north temperate
summer to a south temperate winter. We're discomforted by the
seasonal switch, especially the cold rain, but have no doubts we'll
adjust. The survival of New Zealand's first settlers, on the other
hand, required a much more comprehensive lifestyle adjustment, that
of leaving the year-round warmth of the tropics for a temperate land
with long twilights and seasonal frosts and snows.

This morning, the boys and I learn that the first people to
arrive in New Zealand sailed and paddled long double canoes called
waka that held many travellers. They brought with them from East
Polynesia the starchy corms of *taro*, the tubers of sweet potato or
kūmara, as well as dogs (*kurī*) and rats (*kiore*).[31]

Unlike their homeland, the Land of the Long White Cloud

offered the Polynesians no coconuts, bananas, breadfruit, or pigs. Its dense forests held few fruits and no mammalian sources of protein.[32] To survive, the first settlers learned to store *kūmara* in pits lined with bark to protect the tubers from freezing, and to gather berries and bracken fern roots. They were dog and rat eaters and fished, ate shellfish, hunted seals and birds, and moved from one seasonal hunting or gathering site to another. They cleared land for gardens and wove native plant leaves into clothing, capes, mats, and baskets (*kete*). They had no metal tools or working animals like horses or mules, and their only means of transportation was by foot or by canoe. Yet, they adapted to these islands' conditions amazingly well.[33]

WAR AS A WAY OF LIFE

With time, early Māori tools, decorations, and societies changed. Archaeological artefacts indicate that bone necklaces of East Polynesian design gave way to jade pendants and earrings. The moa-hunters' fish hooks and adzes altered in shape and construction. Weapons of stone, obsidian, and jade unseen in the early culture became prolific. Unfortified villages gave way to settlements protected by hilltop fortresses (stockaded villages) called *pā*. As food resources shrank, due to overpopulation and overexploitation, war became a way of life. The Māori fought to protect or acquire valuable land for gardens, to revenge insults or past defeats, to gain prestige, or to capture slaves who were eaten ceremoniously or simply as a good source of protein.[34]

"Ugh!" My sons grimace in revulsion when I read about cannibalism among the early Māori. Yet, they're intrigued. This country's "pre-European" environment was so different from Canada's, which offered early indigenous peoples large terrestrial mammals like moose, bison, deer, and caribou for food, and fur-bearing land mammals like beaver, lynx, fox, and muskrat for warm clothing.

All day, rivulets formed by raindrops trickle down our kitchen windows. They blur the world beyond our classroom and leave us isolated. Homeschooling in a foreign country holds one danger: loneliness. In Nova Scotia, my family belongs to a local network of homeschooling families that share fieldtrips, special events, and organized physical activities. Outings with other homeschoolers are usually the highlights of our academic year.

Here in Lincoln, although Vilis is surrounded by Kiwis at Landcare, the boys and I feel isolated. Hence, my sons' immediate enrolment in Cubs and Scouts, and hence the skating for Jānis and me, and spring tennis for Dainis. Vilis and I considered enrolling the boys in school and decided against it on the basis that school attendance would cramp our freedom to travel when spontaneous opportunities arise. Thus, in a way we've chosen this loneliness and isolation.

Health. Literature. Algebra. Before our noon break, Dainis completes a *déchirage* art piece depicting a jetliner flying over a map of New Zealand.

AT CUBS during the evening, Jānis's hands transform a five cent piece within a matchbox into a twenty cent piece. Then he creates the illusion of sending a twenty cent piece falling through his head. Like an aspiring Houdini, he presents these magic tricks to the Lincoln Cubs before asking one of the boys to choose a card from a deck. After the boy makes his choice, Jānis identifies the card, without having seen it. Since learning about Kiwi Projects last week, he's practiced these tricks. Now, having overcome the anxiety he radiated a week ago, he basks in his peers' enjoyment.

August 30

WHILE JĀNIS constructs a paper model of Canada's CN Tower and
Dainis cuts sea-creature shapes from bright poster paper, I read to
them of Dutch explorer Abel Janszoon Tasman's expedition from
Java in 1642. An emissary of the Dutch East India Company, Tasman
set out to search for the huge, "missing" southern continent that
seventeenth-century geographers thought necessary to balance the
large land masses of the Northern Hemisphere. His orders were to
find that continent and establish trading with its residents.[35]

Tasman's first sighting of New Zealand was off South
Island's West Coast on December 13, 1642. Stormy conditions
prevented him from making landfall, so he sailed north to a sheltered
bay and spent a day observing the island's peoples, some of whom
paddled double canoes and blew on a shell trumpet. The next day,
when Tasman sent a boat to make contact, warriors in canoes
rammed it and clubbed the men on board, killing four. Tasman
hastily withdrew, naming the anchorage Murderers Bay (now Golden
Bay). He sailed north along the west coast of North Island and made
another attempt to land, but was again routed by hostile Māori.[36]
Thus, he failed to complete his missions.

More than a century passed before another European, the
illustrious British explorer James Cook, set eyes on these islands.
Now, Cook's and Tasman's names grace prominent geographical
features in and around the country. The Tasman Sea separates New
Zealand from Australia. Cook Strait separates New Zealand's North
and South Islands. Abel Tasman National Park occupies South
Island's northwest corner. Aoraki-Mount Cook National Park lies in
the heart of the Southern Alps. It contains Mounts Cook and
Tasman, New Zealand's loftiest peaks.

Other explorers came, too. Jean de Surville landed at

Hokianga in 1769, while Cook was mapping the country. De Surville treated the Māori with brutality. Marion du Fresne, de Surville's countryman, was killed and eaten by the Māori three years later. George Vancouver, Antoine d'Entrecasteaux, and Allessandro Malaspina all visited New Zealand waters in the early 1790s. Yet, it's Abel Tasman and James Cook who stand tallest in New Zealand's history of European exploration.[37]

IN LATE afternoon, Vilis and the boys return from Christchurch. While Jānis skated, Vilis and Dainis bought Cub and Scout handbooks as well as a bicycle tire repair kit in preparation for Dainis's planned cycling adventure. Already, my sons' outings and Scout meetings are the highlights of their weeks here. They've spent too much time in each other's company and too much time indoors due to all the rain. As much as we love each other, the boys are restless and yearning for outdoor activity and more interactions with kids their age.

August 31

THIS COUNTRY'S history is a living thing to my sons. Of all our schooling subjects, it's the one they prize most. Today, I read to them of Nicholas Young, the surgeon's boy onboard the *Endeavour*, Captain Cook's ship. At 2:00 p.m. on October 6, 1769, Nick Young spotted a head of land near present-day Gisborne on North Island and set the stage for the influx of Europeans that would change this country forever. As promised by his captain, the lad's name was given to the land he first saw: Young Nicks Head. Whether he received the other promised reward of a gallon of rum, historians cannot say.[38]

Cook, on a scientific mission sanctioned by the British

Admiralty and the Royal Society, had been sent to Tahiti to observe the transit of Venus across the face of the sun. He was to take measurements that would assist in calculating the distance between the earth and sun. As well, he was instructed to investigate the mysterious land reported by Abel Tasman more than a century and a quarter earlier. He carried several artists and the noted botanists Joseph Banks and Daniel Solander with him on the *Endeavour*. Along with Cook, these men put together a collection of botanical specimens, Māori artefacts, and sketches of landforms, plants, birds, and Māori people that blew the socks off the European scientific elite.[39]

Cook, like Tasman, initially experienced hostility from the Māori. However, after a time, he developed friendly relations with the tribes (*iwi*) he encountered during his half-year circumnavigation of the country, as well as during his two subsequent visits to New Zealand in 1773 and 1777. He prepared detailed cartographic charts that proved the two major landmasses of New Zealand were indeed islands and were definitely not the southern continent Tasman had sought.[40]

Cook came to understand and respect the Māori. He learned to speak some of their language and traded beads, cloth, nails, and axes for fresh food. He also gave the Māori two gifts that improved their diet and reduced their food-gathering time. The first gift was potatoes, which could be grown more easily and farther south than *kūmara*. The second gift was pigs, which offered a large and accessible source of protein.[41]

"Captain Cookers!" The boys laugh when I tell them the nickname given to the pigs Cook left on these islands.[42]

DESPITE THE allure of history, today this old bungalow feels like a prison with bars of rain. By noon, I can't bear its confines any longer. "Let's check out the route for our biking expedition," I suggest to Dainis and Jānis, and we hurry out to the station wagon.

East of Lincoln, puddles and pools of rainwater lie in fields and pastures. Drizzle drips from the sky. We reach Tai Tapu without mishap and soon after, encounter a shallow lake covering the road. After debating whether or not to drive through the water, I take the plunge and do so, stalling once because I shifted into the wrong gear. Water sprays out wildly while the Bomb easily wades the distance, causing the boys to laugh with giddy excitement.

Farther along the road, we encounter an even larger lake with a current running through it. Although swamped by cabin fever, I recognize that attempting to cross that span of moving water would be utter folly. After making an awkward turn, I drive back toward the first lake. From this side, with the car caught between two flooded stretches of road, the span of water looks larger than it did from the other side. With trepidation, I steer the station wagon into it and feel the Bomb slow to a crawl when it hits deeper water. Then we're out and laughing at the thrill of our escapade. Yet my heart pounds with the knowledge that I came close to endangering my sons' safety. Flustered, I approach an intersection and realize I'm driving North American. I steer the station wagon into the correct lane and drive carefully back to Lincoln, my heart still pounding.

This country has unsettled me. Made me question so many things: homeschooling, my ability to deal with unexpected situations, my role here. It's late August, a time when I would be harvesting fruits and vegetables back home, making preserves, filling our freezers with food for the winter. Here, I do none of those things. And I'm unaccustomed to town life, which gives my family the freedom to get around on foot or bicycle, but surrounds us with urban landscapes, rather than the meadows and forests of home. I feel in limbo. Not grounded. Forever putting out feelers. How long does it take to fit in (even a little) in a new country? Will our time in New Zealand be long enough? Or will we look back on these ten months and think of ourselves only as outsiders?

September 3

LINCOLN COMMUNITY Centre wears many costumes. Yesterday, it hosted a craft fair. While perusing vendors' tables, Vilis, the boys, and I were told by a chatty vendor that the "pikelets" we'd read about in Peggy Dunstan's Kiwi memoir, *A Fistful of Summer*, are small, sweet pancakes. I asked the middle-aged vendor, who was selling pikelets, what the correct pronunciation of Milo is (we'd been saying "MEE-lo"), and she set us straight, laughing kindly. 'No, no, you say it, "MY-lo." ' I bought an apron in shades of lemon and turquoise and a large, flat tray made of *rimu* recycled from an old piece of furniture. The tray vendor informed me that *rimu* is one of the most sought-after native trees to supply furniture wood. He also told me that the government recently banned the logging of this rainforest species on public lands.

Dainis and Jānis eyed sausages and popcorn for sale, and Vilis bought a bag of candy floss (cotton candy) to share. The confection's sticky, melting sweetness instantly reminded us of late summer fairs in Canada. The annual Nova Scotia Provincial Exhibition in Truro features a midway with rides, barns filled with 4-H livestock and horses entered in various events, such as barrel racing, as well as ox pulls, displays of vegetables and flowers, jellies and pickles, plus vendors selling corn on the cob, hamburgers, deep-fried pickles, candy apples...and cotton candy.

This morning, the craft fair has been replaced by the least

conservative church I've ever attended, Lincoln Baptist Church. Young adults and children fill many seats. Upbeat, contemporary music pervades the room. Smiling strangers welcome us, in particular, dark-haired Nancy Borrie. Her dry sense of humour and sincere interest put us at ease within minutes. The service, which seems to completely lack ritual, features laughter and a surprising amount of congregational participation. It's as though each member of this congregation truly is a hand or eye or foot in the body of Christ's church.

IN EARLY afternoon, vehicle lights glare like red and white eyes in the blackness of the Christchurch Lyttelton Road Tunnel. Glowing lane markers and the tunnel's tiled walls lead us through 1 900 metres of volcanic rock from Heathcote, in Christchurch, to Lyttelton, Canterbury's most historic port and Christchurch's lifeline to the world's commerce. Completed in 1964, the tunnel offers a direct route to Lyttelton Harbour that avoids the tortuous passage over Lyttelton Volcano's steep slopes and crater rim. The road tunnel parallels a rail tunnel that was drilled and blasted through the volcano's side a hundred years earlier, when settlers filled with dreams of a better life arrived by the shipload from Europe.[43]

The first four such ships to arrive at Lyttelton sailed from England in September of 1850. They carried more than seven hundred passengers destined for the new colony of Canterbury. Passengers wealthy enough to have bought land in the new settlement were classified as "colonists," while those who would work as tradesmen and labourers were classified as "emigrants." Three months of ocean travel transported colonists, emigrants, and their families from encroaching winter in the Northern Hemisphere to summer's blazing heat in the Southern Hemisphere. The *Charlotte*

Jane dropped anchor in Lyttelton Harbour in mid-morning on Monday, December 16, 1850. The *Randolph* soon followed, arriving during the afternoon of the same day. The *Sir George Seymour* released her passengers on December 17. Travellers aboard the *Cressy* had to wait until December 27 to greet their new home.[44]

On our arrival in Lyttelton, the docks, container ships, tugboats, and railway of a modern port town greet us. Houses jut from the rocky hillside and sprawl westward along the shore. Huge cylindrical storage tanks loom like an assortment of white industrial toys overlooking a sheltered collection of jetties and piers. In a marina, graceful yachts rest on serene harbour water.

We hike a coastal track west to Corsair Bay, where the beach is littered with piles of ivory-coloured screw shells and the sand itself is composed, in part, of crushed shells. To the west, rain-fed grass is interrupted by groves of native bush, sunlit peaks, and craggy ridges. Pine trees' flaring branches create dark lace against the vivid green backdrop. A pied shag (cormorant) lands on a branch, the bird's white belly and throat like a dress shirt worn by a man attired in formal black and grey. Red-billed gulls and black-backed gulls cruise over the harbour. We kick at the sand, collect screw shells, and soak up the welcome sunshine we yearned for during recent days of cold, confining rain.

After returning to the car, we trace the harbour shoreline west to the village of Governor's Bay. Vilis steers the car up twisting Dyer's Pass Road to its intersection with Summit Road on the crater rim, where we see a teahouse called Sign of the Kiwi. Last weekend, we explored the ruins of a teahouse at Sign of the Bellbird; today, we observe a fully operational teahouse with stone walls and large windows.

These "Signs" we have so far encountered are two of four

rest stops in the Port Hills that were the brainchildren of Howard Ell, a passionate conservationist who spearheaded the construction of Summit Road in the 1920s and '30s to provide public access to his favourite haunt. The remaining two rest stops are Sign of the Takahē, an ornate teahouse in the Christchurch suburb of Cashmere, and Sign of the Packhorse, a trampers' hut on Mount Bradley Walkway.[45]

Traffic at Sign of the Kiwi is astonishing: cyclists, a half-dozen bikers, and countless cars zoom in four directions at the intersection. It seems all of Canterbury has taken to the heights.

IN MIST ON CRATER RIM WALKWAY

A small hill behind the teahouse draws us to its summit, and we gaze at sunshine battling dark clouds over the harbour. Then we descend the hill and link up with a narrow, muddy section of Crater Rim Walkway that traverses a thrusting peak's flank. Like the day we climbed Gibraltar Rock, we soon abandon the track to scramble toward the peak's summit.

I'm startled by how quickly fog drifts in from the harbour. Within minutes, it shrouds the landscape. Mist follows, sheeting rock surfaces and touching our faces with damp cold. "I think we should go back," I suggest, uneasy in the ever-thickening whiteness.

My sons demure, loathe to relinquish any opportunity to climb.

Vilis stares up toward the summit. "Yeah, we should. We can't even see the top anymore."

Enveloped in mist, we slide down wet rock and grass to the track and hike back to the car. Then Vilis navigates Summit Road's dangerous curves and returns us to the level Canterbury Plain.

At bedtime yesterday, for the first time in two weeks, Vilis and I abandoned our sleeping bags and the hardness of our bedroom floor for a futon bed purchased at a garage sale in Christchurch. This evening, I snuggle into the bed. Its mattress is bliss, and the goose down duvet, pure luxury. *Now* this old bungalow feels like a home.

September 4

THIS MORNING, while builders complete the promised repairs at our rental house, the boys and I again embrace New Zealand history. We learn about sealers and whalers who flocked to this country after news of its marine bounty spread throughout the world in the late 1700s. Although New Zealand was then still primarily a land of birds, its offshore waters provided rich habitat for marine mammals such as fur seals, sperm whales, and right whales.

Gangs of sealers from Australia, Britain, and North America (many of whom were convicts) were dropped off on islands or coastal seal colony sites on the South Island (by this time, the Māori had killed off the North Island seals). While they eked out a rough existence and hoped the ships would return to collect them, the sealers clubbed and shot incredible numbers of seals: bulls, cows, and pups alike. Their pelts were destined for the fashionable felted fur hat industry. In 1806, a single ship's crew harvested 60 000 seal pelts. During one week in 1810, furs worth £100 000 arrived in a single Australian port.[46] This was no sustainable harvest. It was slaughter.

Deep-sea whalers arrived on the scene in 1792 and were followed by bay whalers in the 1820s. The deep-sea whalers targeted gigantic, deep-diving sperm whales. These leviathans provided blubber that was rendered into lubrication and lighting oil, spermacetic wax that was used in candle making, and ambergris that was used to make perfumes. The bay whalers built whaling stations onshore and hunted coastal right whales for oil and bone. At that time, whale bone was in hot demand for umbrella ribs and the stiff supports of constricting corsets European women wore in obeisance to fashion. However, like the sealers who came before them, the bay whalers were too greedy. Their full-scale slaughter of coastal whales left them with nothing to hunt.[47]

Jānis looks at me, an expression of dismay on his face. "Why would they do that? You'd think they would know better."

"All they cared about was money," Dainis tells him.

Of course, that was a different era, and these islands were seen as a treasure trove of natural resources free for the taking. Their bounty brought others, too. Flax traders, seeking tough fibre for the ropes needed on sailing ships, traded with Māori harvesters who gathered coarse flax fibre. Timber cutters logged vast stands of towering, straight-boled *kauri* trees to provide timber for shipbuilding and export. Like the sealers and whalers, these men were rough characters, many of them hailing from Australian penal colonies.[48]

AFTER WE finish schooling, I dry six loads of laundry outdoors in the sunshine and decide there may be hope for New Zealand's weather after all. Jubilant, my sons spend hours on the tennis courts, celebrating their freedom from rain.

September 5

HERALDS OF the Canterbury spring, European skylarks toss clean, tinkling sounds from the sky while I run roadsides near Lincoln. Like the winter wrens who nest in the forest near my home in Nova Scotia, the skylarks sing as though there is no tomorrow, as though God has commissioned them to spill the essence of joy onto the earth this very second.

After my run, I carry their song with me to the rink. When I skate, some of it infuses my blades, which I lift into long, independent strokes.

Chris Street introduces me to sculling. "Push your legs out to the side," he tells me, "and then pull them back in."

The "out" is easy. The "in" is much harder. I feel as though my torso is stranded atop two splayed poles sliding uncontrollably along the ice.

Chris advises, "Squeeze your cheeks together. That'll bring your legs in."

I try it, and it works. So that's how to control my skidding movements! I glance at Chris, and he nods. I've never had a near-stranger refer to my butt cheeks before!

Today the ice is cluttered for the hour-long lesson. So many skaters, and so many names to remember. Petite with frizzy red hair, Daphne. Long, dark hair and laser-focused, Jane. Buxom and confident, Danielle. Blond pixie haircut, Sabrina. And many more. "How are you going?" they ask, offering encouraging smiles as I scull slowly around the rink. Some skate alongside me and ask, "Where're you from?" After our lesson, I sit among these women in Zamboni's, the warm room, and sip hot chocolate and listen to their banter. The sounds of their accents slide into my ears like slippery, bubbly audio-candy. This is precious personal time for me, and practice for unravelling the intricacies of spoken Kiwi.

September 7

POSSIBLE RISKS: bike-car crash, flat tire, dehydration, sunburn, fall off bike.

Precautions: ride on left side of road, use correct hand signals, look both ways before crossing, have pump and bike patches, water bottle, sunscreen, first aid kit.

AT 1:00 P.M., the boys and I cycle out our access road to begin the cycling trip Dainis proposed as his first requirement for the Explorer badge. Beneath an almost clear sky brushed with scattered cloud, Lincoln's quiet streets welcome us. Beyond the township, the Lincoln Tai Tapu Road leads us through farm fields and pastures, the latter grazed by beef and dairy cattle, horses, red deer, and this country's ubiquitous woolly quadrupeds – sheep. Roadside vegetation forms a strung-out collage of shrubs, trees, and exotic grasses. Clumps of pampas grass push shaggy, pale-headed flowering stalks high into the air beside the pavement. Lone pines with flaring branches stand like sentinels at field edges.

Beyond Tai Tapu, we see pastures still flooded from last week's persistent rains and notice flood debris caught high in fences and trees. Adjacent to the road, a pair of graceful mute swans (native to Europe and Asia, these swans are called "mute" because they vocalize much less than other swan species) share a pond with dabbling mallards and two *pūkeko* – marsh birds sporting a sleek black and blue plumage, white derrières, and red face shields. When we pause to admire the swans, the cob, with raised wings and snaking neck, hastens to the fence that separates us. Unwisely, Dainis reaches out to pat him and receives a sharp nip in return. "Ouch!" he yelps, before laughing at the feisty swan.

We picnic beside the pond and then continue cycling east toward the Port Hills' toes. The road traces a hilly hairpin curve, where our legs work hard. Introduced eucalyptus trees tower over us, their bark peeling in ragged strips from thick trunks.

The road loops back toward Tai Tapu too soon, and we leave the gentle heights for flatland pastures edged with hedges. Skylarks sing overhead, and magpies and a spur-winged plover stake out territories in the pastures.

"How are you doing?" I ask the boys when we pause to munch trail mix along the final stretch of the Lincoln Tai Tapu Road.

"Okay," Jānis says, "but my legs are getting tired."

"Yeah." Dainis nods his helmeted head.

Weary and triumphant, we return to Lincoln and celebrate this first expedition's success with ice cream cones from the dairy (convenience store). Afterward, I pedal home slowly. I tackled the two-hour ride after running five kilometres and skating for an hour. Methinks the fitness craze that seems to pervade Canterbury has caught *me* in its grip as well.

EUCALYPTUS TREE BESIDE THE LINCOLN TAI TAPU ROAD

September 8

ON A topographical map, Banks Peninsula resembles a huge, shaggy paw that protrudes from South Island's eastern plain, southeast of Christchurch. Named for Joseph Banks, the brilliant and wealthy "gentleman botanist" who sailed with Captain Cook, the paw, and in particular, its Ōkuti Valley Scenic Reserve, is our tramping destination this afternoon.

The map shows that the northwest reaches of Banks Peninsula enclose Lyttelton Harbour, and that the rest of the peninsula juts thirty kilometres eastward into the Pacific Ocean. Numerous bays and inlets, large and small, bite into the coastline. Lyttelton and Akaroa Volcanoes, which were active 6 million to 11 million years ago and created the peninsula,[49] bump up against each other and overlap somewhat. Lyttelton and Akaroa Harbours resemble blue arms that breach the volcano walls and end in lumpy-fingered hands. Lyttelton Harbour reaches in from the north, and Akaroa Harbour from the south.

I rest the map in my lap as we drive southeast from Lincoln on the Christchurch Akaroa Road. We pass Motukarara, where four-year-old Peggy Dunstan attended the pork butcher's picnic, and then the shore of wide Lake Ellesmere, its surface whipped by the wind. The highway looks as if it will lead us straight into the ocean, then curves eastward in a sharp right angle near Birdlings Flat. It leads us along the western shore of narrow Lake Forsyth, flanked by steep volcanic ridges. If we were to remain on this road, it would carry us to the heart of Banks Peninsula and on to Akaroa, on Akaroa Harbour. However, not far past the end of Lake Forsyth, we turn into Ōkuti Valley.

A stream chuckles alongside us when we begin our upward tramp within Ōkuti Valley Scenic Reserve. Thick bush (native forest) overshadows the track, rich with trees and vines. With my new tree guide in hand, I identify a *kānuka* tree, with its tiny, flat leaves and thin peeling bark, and a *kōwhai*, New Zealand's national tree, with its yellow pea-like blossoms and its twigs lined with pairs of small, rounded leaves.

An exquisite avian voice peals from the bush, startling us. The notes of its song are clear, liquid beauty.

"What is *that?*" Vilis asks in wonder.

With bird guide and binoculars at the ready, I seek the bird, making *pssh* sounds to call it to me. It obliges, and I identify it as a bellbird, a dark olive and yellow songbird endemic to New Zealand. When we hear its song again, it's as though new light has spilled into the world.

IN SHEEP PASTURE ABOVE ŌKUTI VALLEY

The steep, slippery track leads us out of the bush reserve and over a fence to a narrow gravel road. We follow the road upward, sometimes through pine plantations, but more often through windswept sheep and cattle pastures carpeted with dead, wind-beaten grasses angled over fresh green growth.

Where the road gives out, we link up with a quad (all terrain vehicle) trail, and then with cattle and sheep paths that seem to lead us forever upward. Dried logs and stumps of long-dead trees litter the pastures like grey, weathered bones. Black scars mar some of the trunks, the lingering evidence of fires set by Europeans in the late nineteenth century when land was cleared for pasture.[50] We touch the scars and feel history beneath our fingers.

While tramping the hills, we spot a rabbit, magpies, and a dead possum. The dark-furred possum, with its triangular face and thickly furred tail, is cat-sized and was, until its demise, one of 60 million Australian brushtail possums overpopulating New Zealand. Possums were first introduced to New Zealand from Australia in the 1850s for fur farming. Some escaped and others were set free, giving the marsupials free rein to feed voraciously on young tree growth and raid birds' nests for eggs. Nocturnal in their habits and largely unchecked by predators, the possums spread throughout the country. Their numbers skyrocketed until they were declared a pest species almost a hundred years after their introduction. Like stoats, possums are now targeted for extermination.[51]

High on the hills, cold wind buffets us. Dry, open hills sweep in rolling curves in all directions. A grass with leaf stalks like knife blades jabs our legs whenever we brush against it. Each upward sweep of wind-blasted pasture leads to another. In the distance, the silver sheen of Lake Forsyth gleams between steep hillsides patched with neat pine plantations, irregular pockets of bush, and rough upland pastures. Verdant paddocks occupy the valley bottom.

"This hike has one of the best 'view-to-forest ratios' of any I've ever taken," I tell Vilis, using my regular means of ranking hikes in terms of the scenic rewards they offer.

He gazes over the vast panorama. "A person could walk for days in these hills! Camp out on a level stretch atop some hill. You'd just have to carry enough water."

HILLY PASTURES ABOVE ŌKUTI VALLEY

As afternoon wanes, we tramp straight downhill through pastures, rather than retrace the quad track and road to the reserve. The boys romp ahead and collect sheep wool snagged on grasses and stumps. The speed of our descent surprises us: three-and-a-half hours going up, a half hour coming down. This calls for more ice cream.

September 9

WHILE THE sun becomes obscured by cloud, we spend as many hours shopping for camping and tramping supplies in Christchurch malls as we did hiking the hills above Ōkuti Valley yesterday afternoon! We purchase hiking boots for me, a camp stove, rain coats, rubber boots, foam insulation pads, plastic squeeze-tubes for peanut butter and jam, and lightweight dishes. Throughout the mall tedium, an enticement leads us on, for next week we'll travel to Tūtaki Valley in South Island's northwestern Buller District, west of the Southern Alps.

When Vilis heard that three Landcare technicians would be travelling to Tūtaki Valley to dismantle radio-telemetry towers formerly used in a possum removal study, he asked if he could go along to help. Then he asked if Dainis, Jānis, and I could tag along, assuring Landcare that the boys and I are accustomed to camping out and tramping on our own. Excitement filled the house when we heard we had the go-ahead. The trip will be my family's first excursion beyond the Port Hills, Banks Peninsula, and the level agricultural land of the Canterbury Plain. We're keen to see what it brings!

CANADA GEESE are trumpets of the heart, their ringing honks the voice of home as they wing over the tennis courts in Lincoln. Rain soon follows them, chasing Vilis and me from the courts to the bungalow, where Dainis and Jānis delve with rapt attention into a box of LEGO Mindstorms robotics components bought today. Vilis's motive behind the purchase was to encourage the boys to learn to build robots and program computers. This goal, however, runs a distant second to the sheer joy the boys express as they pluck those beloved interlocking pieces of plastic from the box and assemble vehicles of their own imaginative design.

September 11

IN MID-AFTERNOON, the boys and I notice periwinkle flowers

blooming violet against dark green foliage in Liffey Reserve. Starlings and house sparrows peck at grass beneath huge, old English oaks that have not yet unfurled their leaves. Jānis carries a notebook wherein he jots bird species for his latest Kiwi Project, a week-long birding record.

We observe black-and-white magpies perched on oak branches, and female and male blackbirds hopping across the lawn, females brown, males black. A dunnock with a grey nape and collar and a streaked, sparrow-like back sings loudly from a crooked branch. All three are introduced species: the magpie from Australia, and the blackbird and dunnock from Europe. Jānis studies each species and flips through my bird guide's pages until he locates the bird in question and confirms its identity, then he records it. After each stop we follow the path beside the creek, where fantails flit around in thick shrubs. One flash of their long, elegant tails reveals their identity.

"What's that?" Dainis asks excitedly, pointing to the fantails.

Among them flies a shadow that tumbles from branch to leaf-screened branch. The dark bird at last reveals itself. Its body is an exact mimic of the fantails, its tail also a long, elegant fan.

A thrill jolts through me. "It's a black fantail! That colour phase is rare."

"All *right!*" Dainis crows.

Jānis looks up at me with a huge grin on his face. "That's something special for my list!"

It is indeed, and he adds an additional species when, on our return to North Belt, we notice two silvereyes – tiny native songbirds – in a shrub with yellow blossoms at the edge of the yard. Like avian sprites, the small, pert passerines hop quickly from perch to perch, their startling white eye-rings bold invitations to gaze at the rest of their olive, grey, and rust beauty.

September 12

TREES ARE black shadows in ice fog shrouding the Canterbury Plain. The fog's cold, damp breath slides over my skin while I run. In the opaque, humid air, bird songs sound squashed and muted. Hedges loom like dark walls of invisible castles. Blurred vehicle headlights beckon, and then abandon me. Locked in the mist, I run through time, chasing red tail lights that desert me in the white haze.

Later, my kids and I search store after store in Riccarton Mall in Christchurch for warm socks, gloves, and toques (knitted caps), which we'll need for our upcoming two-day adventure in Tūtaki Valley. Finding cold-weather clothing for sale in stores in spring is not an easy task, but we need it. We'll be sleeping in an old farmhouse with no heat in the bedrooms (and we know how that feels!). The boys and I will hike and bird in rain-swept pastures and forests, a sure recipe for hypothermia unless we're properly dressed for the weather. We have rain coats, pants, and rubber boots to keep us dry, but need the gloves, toques, and thick socks for warmth.

After rummaging through piles of end-of-season clothing, my sons and I finally find the necessary items. *Surf's Up* is embroidered on the toque Dainis chooses, and *Not Guilty* on the one Jānis selects. The boys laugh at their dregs of New Zealand's winter clothing.

September 13

AT 7:40 A.M., cold rain spatters us as we dash from the house to a white Landcare 4WD van and toss our backpacks behind the seats. The boys and I scramble onto the rear bench seat, while Vilis climbs into the passenger seat beside Morgan Coleman. The other two technicians, Stephen Hough and Bruce Thomas, will follow in a truck pulling a trailer.

Condensation and raindrops on the van windows impede the boys' and my view as we drive northwest from Christchurch. Frequent window-wipings with our fingers allow us to discern saturated, windswept pastures speckled with sheep, spur-winged plovers, mallards, and numerous *pūkeko* that bob and stride through the downpour. The first paradise shelducks we've seen (females are cinnamon and white; males are cinnamon, grey, and black) waddle through the rain-soaked pastures. In the air, Australasian harriers glide over fields.

Red-haired and talkative, Morgan keeps up a steady stream of conversation with Vilis and tosses thoughtful inquiries or comments to the boys and me. He asks many questions about homeschooling and says that he and his wife Leah hope to have a child soon. He informs us that the pine trees we've seen in plantations and edging farm fields and pastures are *Pinus radiata*, an introduced Californian species that grows rapidly in New Zealand's climate. He says, "A lot of farmers plant them when they're starting out. In twenty-five or thirty years, when they're starting to think about retirement, they harvest them."

Vilis laughs. "Kind of like an RRSP!" (Registered Retirement Savings Plan)

At the Canterbury Plain's western edge, wide, braided rivers spill from the craggy reaches of steep-sided peaks. Within the mountains, the highway clings to rock walls and creeps around hairpin turns. In Lewis Pass, the rain that dogged us from Lincoln is replaced by snow at the higher elevation. Here, amid forested mountains swathed in snow-dusted greenery, New Zealand is suddenly wild. Canterbury's manicured fields and yards have faded to another world.

At Springs Junction, west beyond the pass, we head north through a narrow valley edged with dark, brooding mountains. As rain falls, Morgan tells us that in 1929 the Murchison Earthquake shook these mountains, causing massive landslides. He explains that the earthquake pushed the earth's crust up five metres along a fault line that crosses Maruia River. He pulls off the highway north of Shenandoah to show us Maruia Falls, an elegant spill down a sheer rock wall created by the earthquake.

Beyond Ariki, we angle northeast to Murchison, where our view of rhododendron trees covered with hot pink blossoms is distorted by raindrops trickling down the van's windows. About five kilometres past Murchison and five hours after leaving Lincoln, we turn onto a road that leads us through Mangles Valley and then onto our last road, Tūtaki Road South.

The lush pastures of Oxnams Plain border both sides of the road, creating a long green strip grazed by cattle and sheep and bounded by conical hills cloaked with native forest and exotic pine plantations. Unlike Canterbury, where agriculture dominates the landscape, these pastures are confined to the narrow valley bottom and appear wilder, less controlled.

After unloading our packs at the old farmhouse rented by Landcare, we retrace ten kilometres of road to a pasture where a radio-telemetry tower supports an alien-looking silver antenna. While Morgan, Stephen, and Bruce begin to dismantle the tower, Vilis accompanies the boys and me uphill into a red beech forest.

The forest's floor is draped with mosses so lush they create velour blankets on stumps and logs. Other mosses hang like soft green tinsel from branches of young trees. These beeches (*Nothofagus fusca*), with their ovoid, toothed leaves, are one of four species of

Southern Hemisphere beeches that grow in colder or less-fertile habitats in New Zealand.[52] In this forest, abundant young beeches rise slim and tall, reaching for light beneath the dense canopies of mature beeches with trunks so thick and dark they could be disordered columns of a shadowed Parthenon.

RED BEECH FOREST

Miniscule, beneath the towering trees, my family lounges on mossy-stump thrones and hams it up for mossy hair photographs. This verdant forest's ambience is completely opposite to that of the dry hills we hiked in Ōkuti Valley five days ago. There, we tramped primarily through brown sheep pastures strewn with dead tree trunks and stumps. Here, we're surrounded by such an abundance of moist forest growth, the very air is hung with green.

IN RED BEECH FOREST, TŪTAKI VALLEY

Vilis points to a black substance covering the lower trunks of many of the young beeches. "What's this black stuff?"

I hazard a guess. "Charcoal?"

"The trees don't look burned."

"No, and it looks sticky."

We see more of the black substance coating stumps and trunks, its wet darkness, a vivid contrast to the forest's green. Fantails flit around us, and a male tomtit – a tiny, black-headed songbird – perches nearby as though to explain the source of the trees' black footings.

Two hours pass like minutes. At last, we exit the forest and meet Morgan, who has come looking for any lost Canadians.

"It's a fungus," he explains when Vilis asks about the black on the beech trees. "It feeds on honeydew, a sweet liquid produced by scale insects that feed on the trees' sap. The liquid drips down the trunks and the fungus grows all over it."

That explains the black substance's wet appearance and the way it seems to ooze from tree trunks onto the adjacent forest floor.

We hike downhill through bracken fern to the pasture and telemetry tower. The boys and I leave Vilis and the other men to dismantle the remaining equipment while we saunter toward the farmhouse along Tūtaki Road South.

Muddy from recent rain and spattered with cow patties at cattle crossings, Tūtaki Road South is a narrow gravel lane through the middle of nowhere. Hills crowd the skyline to the north and south. Cattle and sheep share roadside pastures with shelducks and mallards, magpies and spur-winged plovers. Two slender grey, white-faced herons stab at prey in flooded depressions. Flocks of European goldfinches swirl like gold-and-red-flecked dust devils before streaming across the sky. Dark clouds billow above us, and mist sweeps in to touch our faces before giving way to mottled sunshine.

"This has to be the most peaceful road in New Zealand," I tell Dainis and Jānis, while we walk down its center. They agree. We've covered most of the ten kilometres back to the farmhouse and have seen only one pickup truck. It's no hardship to continue walking, and we grin with delight at the telemetry crew's surprise at finding us so near the house. We hop into the van for the last kilometre and spill out into the farmhouse yard, ravenous.

Bruce prepares a tasty tea culminating with a delicious frozen, trifle-like dessert. After the meal, rain pounds onto the farmhouse roof. We gather in the small, worn living room where Morgan lights a fire in the fireplace to ward off night's encroaching cold. He places pine cones on the hearth to demonstrate to the boys how heat causes the serotinous cones to open and release their seeds. Again he's talkative, as is dark-haired, portly Bruce. Stephen, as red-haired as Morgan, speaks little, his presence quiet and gentle in the background.

Bruce asks about our avian sightings, so I tell him of the shelducks and herons, the goldfinches and mallards and plovers. "Oh, yes, and fannies." As soon as I heard what I said, I add, "Sorry, I mean fantails."

Bruce shakes his head gently. "No, you're all right. 'Fannie' is acceptable for the bird."

It's a quirk of Kiwi life that New Zealanders create diminutives by dropping word endings and replacing them with *ie*. Hence, the biscuits or cookies that become "biccies," the hot water bottles that become "hotties," and the fantails that become "fannies."

At first, the boys are shy in the presence of the three technicians. They delve into copies of *Weapons and Warfare* published a quarter century ago and left at the farmhouse. Dainis tells me that the Sopwith Camel was king of the skies during World War I's aerial battles.[53] Later, my sons play cards and, with encouragement from the Landcare crew, Jānis's shyness evaporates sufficiently for him to demonstrate the magic tricks he performed at Cubs. I'm thankful for the men's kindness.

Before bedtime, I step out into cold night air and stroll to the yard's edge to use the "long drop," the New Zealand equivalent of a Canadian outhouse. Above me, a huge white moon soars in a star-studded sky.

Back in the farmhouse, Vilis, the boys, and I bundle up in layers and scoot into our sleeping bags in a bedroom filled with an all-too-familiar chill. After Dainis and Jānis snuggle down deep in their bags, I catch glimpses of their toque-covered heads. *Surf's Up. Not Guilty.*

September 14

THIS MORNING, frost captures every grass stem and shrub twig in its scintillating grip. Ground fog hangs above pastures and mountainsides. It billows upward in white clouds that dissipate in blue sunlit sky.

TŪTAKI ROAD SOUTH THROUGH TŪTAKI VALLEY

After breakfast, Vilis and the Landcare technicians drive away to dismantle the second radio-telemetry tower. Before heading out on a hike, the boys and I study several muttering *tūī* – blackish-brown birds with iridescent flashes of green and two distinctive white balls of feathers hanging from their throats. *Tūī* are members of the honeyeater bird family and, like other honeyeaters, they feed on nectar or berries. Often, they twist open flowers to delve deep into their sweet depths. We watch the *tūī* in the farmyard repeatedly plunge their beaks into shrub catkins. Jānis and I add this new species to our notebooks, then the three of us cross the road to a pasture and follow a small river upstream.

Boulder-studded and decorated with white riffles, the river rushes along the valley bottom. Its shoreline is a tangle of old grasses combed by recent floodwaters. To the south, distant sheep are visible as white specks pastured on grassy ledges and rounded hills below dark green forests. Snow gleams on faraway mountains. Paradise shelducks' bright colours stand out against green and tawny grasses in the pastures. Three dead, bloated ewes and a Hereford cow lie near the river's edge. They likely drowned in recent floods or something went wrong during the birthing process.

TŪTAKI VALLEY PASTURE

Repelled by the dead livestock, the boys and I abandon the riverside pasture and cross the road. We thrash our way upward through bracken fern (the roots of which were once a staple food for the Māori) to the foot of a pine plantation on a steep slope behind the farmhouse. Two male tomtits and a half-dozen *tūī* fly near us to investigate. The *tūī's* white neck tufts dangle like fluffy, paired pendants.

Weary from our first excursion, we return to the farmhouse.

Later, fortified by a snack and a rest on the farmhouse's airy, east-facing veranda, my sons and I walk the most peaceful road in New Zealand toward the second telemetry tower. Birdsong fills the air, and the long valley and mountains entice us onward.

TŪTAKI VALLEY

When the telemetry crew meets us on the road, Vilis joins the boys and me for the return stroll to the farmhouse. I point out birds, and Dainis and Jānis guffaw with delight as they hurl stones into cow patties and mud.

Back at the farmhouse, Vilis and the technicians load the

vehicles with telemetry equipment. The boys and I lounge on the veranda out of the way, soaking up the peace of this place and knowing we'll never return. Across the valley, a harrier soars on a thermal, spiralling high into the sky.

September 15

GIBRALTAR ROCK'S clean, upswept profile beckons as Dainis and I cycle toward Tai Tapu after a morning of unpacking, chores, and unsettled schooling. At first my sons repeatedly complained about their assignments, yet later completed their work with full cooperation.

Today my family is sandwiched between adventures. Yesterday evening, we returned from Tūtaki Valley in time for Dainis to attend the last forty-five minutes of Scouts, a treasured time of interaction with his peers. Tomorrow, we'll tramp Godley Head Track east of Christchurch.

Blustery winds shove against our bicycle wheels and cause us to swerve about in the lane. The sun beats down, banishing all remnants of the recent cold rain.

"My legs and feet are sore from all that walking at Tūtaki," I tell Dainis when we reach Tai Tapu.

He nods. "Mine, too."

In a wool-carding shop that caught my eye on our first visit to Tai Tapu a month ago, Dainis and I receive a respite while I choose skeins of light and dark brown yarn spun from sheep's wool and culled possums' fur. In this case, the culling of possums has benefited not only the environment, but entrepreneurs as well. Although the yarns' cozy softness tempts me to linger, I know Vilis must return to work after lunch and Jānis needs supervision. Dainis and I leave the shop, wince at the sun's glare, and mount our bicycles for the homeward battle against the wind.

September 16

SURF POUNDS onto black sand, its rolling crests ridden by surfers and sea kayakers drawn to Taylor's Mistake Beach. This dark beach marks the base of Godley Head, a thumb of land projecting into the Pacific Ocean north of Lyttelton Harbour.

"Why is it called Taylor's *Mistake*?" Dainis asks.

"Apparently a Captain Taylor sailed into this bay thinking it was Lyttelton Harbour," I relate. "He grounded his ship."[54]

The boys snigger in unison, "That was some mistake!"

Brightly painted baches (cottages edging the beach) stand with their windows overlooking the ocean. Some are plain. Others display contrasting trim and perch amid rock gardens aflame with mounds of purple, orange, and yellow flowers. We hike across the black sand, past the baches, and up onto rounded, grassy hills. Cliffs plunge to the ocean at the hills' base, their ledges stained with whitewash squirted by rock pigeons, black-backed gulls, and spotted shags.

"Do you see the spotted shags' two crests?" I ask Jānis, who has already noted the gulls and pigeons.

Through his binoculars, Jānis studies the upright-standing seabirds. "Yes. And I see the black spots on their backs."

Godley Head Track, our tramp du jour, is no more than a narrow dirt trail that meanders through grazed, treeless pastures. The first section parallels Godley Head's scalloped, northern coastline and is exposed and dry. For the second day in a row, surprising heat tosses a stifling cloak over Canterbury. We rest often, sipping water while sitting on grass tussocks and listening to the songs of introduced grassland birds: skylark, yellowhammer, goldfinch.

GODLEY HEAD TRACK

"I read that the cliffs of the north coast of Godley Head contain sea caves," I mention, "and that people lived in some of the caves in the late eighteen hundreds. One fellow even had a piano in his cave." [55]

The boys laugh in surprise. "How would he get it there?" Jānis asks.

"By boat."

Beyond Boulder Bay with its isolated cottages, the track leads inland and up. We hike to its highest point and are rewarded with spectacular views of Lyttelton Harbour and Banks Peninsula to the south. The rich blue harbour matches the sky, and beyond the water, steep-sided hills rise up, dull green and creased by tree-lined valleys.

Dainis and Jānis race downhill, more interested in a cluster of concrete buildings on the slope below us than in the view. According to our tramping guidebook, the blocky structures are remnants of abandoned World War II military batteries, barracks, messes, and a magazine.[56] Dainis stands on an exposed round floor with a gun mount in its centre and a 360-degree firing view. "Look at this battery!" He clutches the gun mount. "You could shoot in any direction!"

"It looks like this is where the soldiers slept," Jānis calls from the doorway of the old barracks. Inside, bunk frames are fastened to cement walls.

We cast quick looks at the remaining squat structures, then continue on the track. The boys are eager to explore a 110-metre tunnel dug through coastal rock to allow access to two searchlights on the shore. They romp ahead and leap from the path onto mounds of densely twigged shrubs with tiny leaves. "What are these shrubs?" Jānis asks.

"I know!" Dainis yells. "They're 'sit-able' shrubs!" He flings his arms wide and jumps up and onto another resilient clump.

I convince the boys to make a brief side trip to a lookout over rocky cliffs, where we watch hundreds of red-billed gulls mill and screech. The gulls' grey and white elegance is a stark contrast to dark, precipitous cliffs and a grassy slope on which many of the birds rest.

A few minutes later, we plunge downhill toward the tunnel's

entrance. Inside, moisture squelches beneath our shoes in the darkness. Our voices echo. Small, regularly spaced side tunnels provide peep holes that offer enough light for safe travel.

"I like that it's long," Jānis says, the thrill of mystery in his voice.

"And that it's dark," Dainis adds excitedly.

Too soon, we reach the tunnel's end and scramble among huge boulders down to a rock-strewn shore where searchlights beamed brilliant light across the harbour's neck as they searched for enemy vessels.

After we return through the exciting tunnel, the remainder of the tramp is a struggle. Jānis, who rose at 4:50 a.m. in order to be on the ice at 6:00 a.m., wilts in the afternoon heat. I carry his pack and boost his butt up steep inclines. Dainis realizes he's lost his watch somewhere along the path, so he and Vilis backtrack in search of it before giving up. We trudge over the hump of Godley Head and cut across tussocked slopes on a mountain bike trail, pausing often to rest. Finally, we tackle the downward track that returns us, five hours after our start, to the cliffs above Taylor's Mistake Beach.

BACK AT the bungalow on North Belt, Dainis whispers in my ear and then rushes off to the Four Square Supermarket. In the study, purple paper rustles as Jānis and I wrap gifts. Then I spread chocolate fudge icing over the chocolate cake I baked this morning while Jānis and Vilis were at the rink.

Dainis returns from the store and, with a secretive smile, places slim candles on the cake and lights them. "Happy Birthday to you!" the boys and I sing to Vilis as I place the cake on the table before him.

"Blow out your candles," the boys say.

Vilis puffs out a huge breath. The flames falter, then flare to life again.

Dainis and Jānis burst out laughing. "Try again," Dainis encourages.

Repeatedly, Vilis sucks in huge lungfuls of air to blast the candles, but they stubbornly remain lit. His face turns red with effort, and our boys laugh harder and harder.

"*Where* did you get these candles?" my husband pants.

"At the grocery store," Dainis responds innocently.

Finally, the boys and I relent and snuff out the never-blow-out candles Dainis spotted at the Four Square Discount last week. We can't have Vilis concluding that, at the age of forty-five, he's too old and feeble to blow out his birthday candles.

WHEN I read today's issue of Christchurch's *The Press*, I see that the Sydney Olympics are front-page news. So is the filming of movie scenes for *The Two Towers*, based on J. R. R. Tolkien's second book in *The Lord of the Rings* trilogy. A photo shows steep-walled buildings on craggy rocks, with a snow-dusted peak in the background. This is Edoras, the fictional crown city of Rohan, land of the horse lords. The movie set was built in six months on windswept Mount Sunday, a massive rock outcrop in grassland beyond Ashburton Gorge in west Canterbury. For the next two weeks, that rugged landscape will be crawling with camera crews, celebrities, and extras before it reverts to grazing land owned by Mount Potts Station.[57]

September 17

THIS AFTERNOON, my family slogs through sodden pasture on the shore of Lake Ellesmere, seeking new bird species to lengthen Jānis's and my lists. The lake is located about twelve kilometres south of Lincoln and is a huge shallow body of brackish water separated from the Pacific Ocean only by the narrow gravel barrier of Kaitorete Spit. The Māori name for the lake is Te Waihora, "The Spreading Water," which is certainly apt. Although Lake Ellesmere is New Zealand's fifth largest lake, it used to cover (before Europeans tamed the Canterbury Plain for farming) twice the area it does now. It's a cherished *mahinga kai* (garden) of the local Māori, the Ngāi Tahu. In pre-European times, the tribe regulated the lake's volume to encourage fish and waterfowl stocks.[58]

AT LAKE ELLESMERE

Today, the lake is alive with birds. Black swans look like dark ships on the water and dark aircraft in a blue cloudless sky. The air resonates with their rich-toned trumpeting. A few white mute swans keep company with the black swans, and Canada geese and mallards glide in flotillas dwarfed by their majestic cousins. Overhead, pied stilts (long-legged waders of the avocet and stilt bird family) trail red legs that suggest dancers' stockings beneath black-and-white dresses. A black-fronted tern, grey and white with a black cap, hovers in the air and repeatedly dives to the water's surface to capture prey. *Pūkeko* skulk among the reeds, and white-faced herons stand patiently and unleash motion in stabbing flashes. The water shivers from wind touches and bird movement, the air flecked with avian sound.

Weary from our Godley Head tramp yesterday, we turn away from the lake after two hours. As our rubber boots slop over saturated ground, skylarks flutter in the sky above us, madly singing their joyous songs of mating. And Jānis's and my bird lists are longer.

September 18

THIS MORNING, as part of schooling, Jānis and Dainis painstakingly stretch a thread over a map of Godley Head, fitting it to each curve and twist of the tracks we tramped in order to estimate the total distance we hiked. They straighten the thread, measure its length, and with the aid of the map legend, transpose that length into the distance travelled. The resulting estimate is slightly less than eight kilometres. In Saturday's heat, the distance seemed so much longer.

IN MID-AFTERNOON, Jānis studies a small, brightly coloured bird on the ground in Liffey Reserve. It's a species he doesn't yet have on his Kiwi Project list.

"We saw flocks of those at Tūtaki while walking along the road," I remind him. "And we saw a dead one on the roadside in West Melton."

He flips through my bird guide, which I've opened to the passerine (songbird) section, and locates the illustration of the European goldfinch. Its colourful red, white, and black head and black, yellow, and white wings distinguish it from any of the other birds. "Is it a goldfinch?" he asks.

"Yes."

"Good! That's twenty-nine."

We continue searching along the park paths, first on one side of the creek and then on the other. Tomorrow evening at Cubs, Jānis will present his list, so he, Dainis, and I are on a last quest for more species. Movement in tall shrubs next to the creek draws our attention.

"That's a fantail," Jānis states.

Dainis points. "And there's the black one!"

Like two dancers performing an elegant and erratic aerial ballet, the fantails tumble through the shrubs. Their long tails fan as they gain perch after perch. One bird is soot on the wing. Its black beauty is a flash of night against the foliage, its dark presence a shadowy alter-identity of its mate, a common pied fantail. Oblivious to our presence or unconcerned by it, the fannies drop from the shrubs to the shallow creek where they bathe with splashing wings and bring laughter to our lips. Caught in sunlight and shadows, the fantails are lovely beyond measure and a little bit clumsy. I know New Zealand's national bird is the kiwi, but fantails have stolen our hearts.

September 19

THE BOYS' attentiveness soars when Vilis begins reading aloud from *A River Rules My Life*, Mona Anderson's memoir of her adventures as the wife of a South Island sheep rancher who owned a 100 000-acre station beside the Wilberforce River in the rugged mountains south of Arthur's Pass. Mona first crossed the Wilberforce on a huge old wagon pulled by five draft horses, her wedding gifts jouncing beside her as she crossed the boulder-strewn river to get to her new home at the base of Mount Algidus. Her words introduce Dainis and Jānis to the unkempt, threadbare teamster, Jim, who cared meticulously for his equine charges; to the old cook, Jack, who never measured his ingredients; and to the challenges faced by a city bride on a remote mountain station in 1939.[59] I don't mention that Anderson's memoir is another thread in the tapestry of New Zealand's history and culture. It's enough that Dainis and Jānis soak up every word.

September 21

WITH DESPERATE speed, Vilis, the boys, and I pull on clothes, push food into our mouths, and race to the car. I thank God for the empty streets of early morning as Vilis drives to the airport faster than I've ever seen him drive. He has a plane to catch and set his alarm for the wrong time. Nonetheless, we arrive at the airport ten minutes before his flight to Wellington is scheduled to depart. He sprints for the entrance doors and his rendezvous with Andrea Byrom, who is undoubtedly already on board. After arriving in Wellington, he and Andrea will drive north to Ōwhango and the Tongariro Forest Conservation Area. There, Vilis will acquaint himself with the stoat research site and the studies being conducted.

Back home, the boys and I search the house from entrance to back door and from kitchen to bedroom, hoping to find Jānis's binoculars, which went astray on the weekend. In the end, we conclude that they're gone, lost somewhere amid the tussocks on Godley Head – our second loss to that dry, mounded thumb of land touching Lyttelton Harbour.

Due to our disrupted morning, we carry schooling into the afternoon. To create an illustration for a New Zealand historical timeline the boys have begun, Jānis draws a highly decorated Māori war canoe (*waka taua*), its stern rising tall and graceful on his paper. He bases his drawing on a sketch done by Sydney Parkinson, one of the artists onboard Cook's ship *Endeavour*.[60] Through our studies, my sons and I have learned that New Zealand's first settlers were great seafarers who built beautifully carved canoes and that, as Jānis prints above this illustration, *Maoris were cannabalistic, kept slaves, and were warlike.* [61] He, like Dainis, is impressed and repelled by these traits.

September 22

TO CREATE more illustrations for our historical timeline, the boys rub soft black pencil onto paper placed over a half-dozen New Zealand coins. Dainis rubs the *kōtuku* or white heron (sacred to the Māori) from the two-dollar coin. He uses it and a sketch of a three-metre giant moa to accompany his statement on the timeline's first page: *New Zealand is 2 000 kilometres from other lands, and has been isolated for many millions of years. Because of this isolation, mammals never evolved* (here), *causing it to become a land of birds.*

Jānis traces the brown kiwi from the twenty cent coin and the spotted kiwi from the dollar coin to accompany his sketches of three of New Zealand's five kiwi species. Then he writes of pre-human times: *Many birds of New Zealand are flightless because there were no mammalian predators.*

Page three is a collage of both boys' work, illustrated with pencil crayon sketches of silver tree fern and cabbage tree (the tree with the wildly untidy head of dagger-like leaves we encountered on Holdsworth Track two weeks ago). This page also includes Dainis's five cent coin rubbing and pencil sketch of a *tuatara*, an ancient lizard species now found only on New Zealand's offshore islands. *There are some kinds of plants in New Zealand that haven't changed since the time of the dinosaurs,* Dainis writes. *Tuatara is the same.*[62]

When the timeline scoots ahead to the arrival of humans, Dainis illustrates that information with a rubbing of an intricately carved Māori war mask lifted from a ten cent coin. Then, leap-frogging over the page devoted to Abel Tasman that Jānis is preparing, he captures the image of James Cook's ship *Endeavour* from a fifty cent coin.

As we walk the streets of Lincoln, this country's history and fauna jingle in our pockets.

During the evening, my sons and I drive to the airport – at a much more sedate pace than Vilis drove yesterday morning – to collect my husband on his return from North Island. "Why are you wearing sweatpants?" I ask Vilis after the boys and I greet him with hugs.

He laughs. "Oh, I fell off the back of a quad into a hole, so my jeans got covered in mud." He tells us that the tracks in the Tongariro Forest Conservation Area were logging roads twenty-five or thirty years ago, and that since logging was banned, most of the old roads have deteriorated into narrow trails pitted with mudholes. "We were going uphill, two on a quad, which we weren't supposed to do. The driver had to hit the acceleration hard, and I wasn't holding on tight, so I tumbled off the back."

He regales us with more stories – how he had to leap off the back of a quad when it began to bog down in a deep mudhole on Mud Track, and how he and Andrea and Wendy Ruscoe, a rat researcher, flew over the study area. The two women discussed the different areas they could see and compared them to a map. "To me, it was just all green," he says.

So. *Green. Quads. Mud.* That's how Vilis describes where we'll work for a month in December and January. *Should be interesting.*

September 23

DRESSED IN windproof pants and jacket, Jānis crouches on a slanted expanse of pebbles at Birdlings Flat, southeast of Lincoln. He drags a pile of wave-smoothed stones onto his lap and eagerly searches for green among the grey. Beyond him, the silvery-grey beach extends east to the base of red cliffs used by rock pigeons as nesting sites. To the west, Kaitorete Spit forms a thin wedge of gravel separating Lake Ellesmere from the ocean. We've come to Birdlings Flat seeking New Zealand jade, also known as nephrite, greenstone, or *pounamu*.

Jānis saves one or two pebbles that show a greenish hue when wet. These, he shoves into pockets bulging with previously collected pebbles. Soon, he empties his pockets into his daypack. We amble toward the red cliffs, plucking jade and other brightly coloured stones from among countless grey pebbles. The jade varies in colour from light to dark green, its heart often a swirl of greens and milky white.

NEW ZEALAND JADE

The nephrite form of jade found on New Zealand's South Island is a calcium magnesium silicate mineral that contains small amounts of iron, resulting in its different hues of green. Formed deep within the earth, jade's presence aboveground is the result of mountain-building processes that formed the Southern Alps. Erosion by glaciers and rivers released jade from surrounding rock and introduced it into glacial debris and riverbeds, with some pieces travelling from the Alps to the ocean and ending up on coastal beaches like the one at Birdlings Flat.[63]

In bygone centuries, Māori crossed mountains to find jade, fought over it, traded it, considered it a symbol of authority, and exchanged weapons or heirlooms made from it during peace ceremonies. In a land with few metals, the stone they called *pounamu* became their material of choice for tools, weapons, and ornaments. To this country's first peoples, South Island was Te Wāhi Pounamu, "The Place of Greenstone," a name later changed to Te Wai Pounamu, "The Greenstone Waters." Jade remains a significant aspect of Māori culture, with professional carvers producing traditional designs showcased throughout the country.[64]

Tired of jade-hunting and inspired by the beach's steep slant and loose stones, Dainis dives onto his belly and toboggans down the incline like a penguin on Antarctic ice. Jānis is quick to follow. Again and again, the boys dive and slide, their laughter pealing out and attracting curious glances from onlookers.

When their bellies complain from the rough treatment, we head for the car, and when Jānis labours beneath his pack, Vilis hoists it onto his own shoulder, saying, "This must weigh thirty pounds!"

We pile into the station wagon and drive Bayley's Road toward Kaitorete Spit's thin tip. Cattle pastures bordering the road have become display grounds for skylarks, magpies, and plovers. The birds' enmeshed voices combine sweetness, hoarseness, and craziness into a wild tango. At the road's end, we explore pale, fine-grained sand dunes and a beach of coarse black sand. When we remove our shoes to test the Pacific Ocean, it washes cold over our feet, winter's touch strong in its sliding sheen.

Later, we join Oliver Sutherland (head of Lincoln's Landcare Research branch) and his wife Ulla for a gracious meal at their home in Christchurch. Bespectacled and sporting a crew cut, Oliver is charming and urbane. Ulla is an organizational wizard, her talents ranging from nurturing the terraced gardens of her front yard to preparing a delicious repast featuring green-shelled mussels, roast lamb, new potatoes, and a dessert of flaky biscuits topped with thickened cream and Swedish cloudberry jam.

After our meal, while adults converse, Dainis and Jānis watch the Sydney Olympics on television and try to produce deep, thrumming sounds by blowing air into Oliver's didgeridoo, an Australian Aboriginal musical instrument consisting of a long wooden tube. Then they doze in the cushioned comfort of the living room. Long hours have passed since they belly-tobogganed down the pebble beach, their laughter pealing into the coastal air.

September 24

RED DEER graze in an emerald pasture near Tai Tapu. The fifty or sixty animals straggle toward a distant line of trees beneath billowing clouds. Their sleek, leggy bodies seem too wild to be confined by fences.

This species, long the prey of nobility in England, is yet another mammal introduced to New Zealand by wealthy colonists in the mid-1800s to provide sport. However, by 1922, an estimated 300 000 red deer grazed grasses and browsed shrubs and young trees throughout New Zealand, damaging or destroying potential forests. After their official designation as pests, deer were shot by the thousands by government-paid cullers, many of whom were World War II and Vietnam War veterans. The latter sometimes took out their quarry from helicopters. Once the deer population plummeted, some of the remaining animals were captured by enticing them into camouflaged pens or by bulldogging them from helicopters. Those captive deer provided the breeding stock for red deer farming.[65]

We leave the deer to their pasture and drive up into the hills behind Tai Tapu, seeking a track not closed due to lambing. Thunder rumbles, and lightning rips open dark clouds. The storm sweeps rain and wind across pastures and into the hills, putting an end to our hiking plans. We spot a pair of wild turkeys (another introduced bird) in long grass beside Gerkins Road. The tom puffs out his nearly black feathers, drops his speckled wings in an eye-catching display, and raises his tail in a stiff, white-tipped fan of challenge. He asserts his dominance with loud gobbles while his hen slips away through wind-curved grasses.

September 25

THE EUROPEAN *traders wanted pigs, potatoes, flax, timber. The Maoris wanted guns, axes, gunpowder,* writes Dainis on our historical timeline, beside his sketch illustrating a Māori and a Pākehā (European or Caucasian) offering goods for trade. Jānis adds, *25 bags of spuds were traded for one musket.* He draws a pyramid of potato sacks beside a lone musket. Dainis tacks on, *Hongi Hika was a Maori chief who could speak English. When he came back from England he had bought 300 muskets. They started the musket wars.* [66]

DISEASES AND MUSKETS TAKE THEIR TOLL

Historians estimate that the Māori population was at least 200 000 strong before Europeans arrived in New Zealand in the late 1700s. In the early 1800s, the Māori were confident in their warrior prowess and dominated Europeans in strength and number.[67] However, by the late 1830s, the Māori population had plummeted by 40 percent, decimated by foreign diseases and massive tribal warfare.[68] By 1896, only about 42 000 Māori remained alive; four-fifths of the "Pre-European" population had perished.[69]

Historians blame Europeans for both causes of the Māori population crash. While Pākehā offered trading goods (the most sought-after of these were muskets, axes, nails, blankets, and red cloth – red being used by the Māori to mark *tapu* or sacred objects) they also brought alcohol and infectious diseases such as whooping cough, smallpox, and measles, to which the Māori had no immunity.[70] Unscrupulous land grabbers convinced Māori to sell their lands for a few European wares. Colonizers surveyed out blocks of land to be bought at a lottery in London without regard for the Māori villages, *pā,* and burial grounds encompassed within the lots. Australian squatters with sheep appeared in droves and staked out pasturelands they didn't own.[71]

As a result of the influx of Europeans, skirmishes between Māori and Pākehā escalated, as did tribal warfare fanned by the availability of guns.[72] An estimated 40 000 Māori were killed in the Musket Wars, during which cannibal feasts escalated into never-before-seen orgies of excess.[73] Historian Keith Sinclair wrote that, "Europe came to Aotearoa like nothing so much as the plague."[74]

The trading era of the early to mid-1800s to which the boys refer was a wild and bloody span in New Zealand's history. It earned these islands the nickname "Cannibal Isles"[75] and a reputation as one of the Pacific's most dangerous destinations.[76]

Hongi Hika was a major instigator of the Musket Wars' rampant bloodshed in the early nineteenth century. In 1821, on his return from a trip to England with the missionary Thomas Kendall, with whom he'd worked to create a Māori-English dictionary, the great North Island chief traded gifts he'd received for muskets and then went hunting old Māori tribal enemies. He and his musket-armed warriors killed thousands of them.[77]

Te Rauparaha, another powerful North Island chief, killed many Māori enemies as well. In 1830, he even arranged to have a British captain ferry him and his warriors all the way to Akaroa on Banks Peninsula. In exchange for a cargo of flax, the captain, John Stewart, helped the chief and his warriors massacre a *pā's* (fortress's) entire population. Stewart then ferried the warriors and their human meat supply home to North Island.[78]

This bloody history takes a toll on the boys' and my emotions, so we vault from violent past to sunlit present through flexibility exercises and then tennis, slugging balls over the net at the Lincoln courts. Afterward, we sip cold drinks while the radio news reports a severe outbreak of salmonella bacterium in house sparrows. First released in this country by the Auckland Acclimatisation Society in 1867, house sparrows provided the sound of home for hardy European settlers. That comfort, however, was soon replaced by dismay and alarm. The sparrows, unchecked by natural predators, multiplied and feasted in grain fields the settlers had laboriously cleared and planted.[79] Now, house sparrows are a potential source of disease to humans, since salmonella bacteria can be transmitted from infected birds to humans through bird droppings.

September 26

OUR RADIO has become the voice of New Zealand. The names of towns, rivers, and politicians are becoming more familiar, and the idiosyncrasies of Kiwi life have begun seeping into our consciousness as our days in this country slip by. This morning, we hear that major highways on North Island are closed due to ice and snow dumped overnight by a late spring storm.

Today's weather in Lincoln is the dregs of that storm, or perhaps drippings from a sky-cauldron that churns with rain, hail, cloud, and sun spilling haphazardly over its brim. Vilis and the boys program LEGO Mindstorms robotic vehicles while I catch up on paperwork and stroll nearby streets between downpours of rain and barrages of hail. The oaks in Liffey Reserve that were leafless a week ago show signs of unfurling fresh, new foliage. Beside Lincoln High School's driveway, masses of red and yellow tulips wave in the wind like can-can dancers' ruffled dresses.

In early afternoon, I drive Jānis to a farm located on the agricultural plain north of Lincoln. Along with several other boys, he's been invited to spend the afternoon with Jason, a member of the Lincoln Koreke Cub Pack. Shy and excited, Jānis heads off on his adventure while I chat briefly with Jason's mother, Sue, in her immaculate yard. "What kind of shrub is that?" I ask, pointing to a small tree flaunting blossoms that resemble fried eggs. The same blossoms have appeared in the hedge bordering our yard.

"It's a camellia," Sue says. Before rushing off to work, she generously takes a few minutes to show me other camellia varieties she owns, some with single blossoms like the fried-egg variety and others with frilly, double blossoms.

When I return to the farm in late afternoon, Dainis, who earlier played tennis with other beginners on the Lincoln courts, accompanies me. He gladly accepts an invitation to join the younger boys for a wagon ride. When Jason's father and the boys return, excitement flares in my sons' voices. They tell me they saw peacocks and a possum hole in a tree. I see their enthusiasm and know they've experienced a completely different adventure from our family hikes and homeschooling investigations. A new door has opened for them, one of acceptance and the outstretched hand of friendship in a land far from home.

September 28

LIKE AN elongated diamond or a night-swan in flight, the Southern Cross (flag emblem of New Zealand and Australia) hangs in the darkness over R. F. Joyce Observatory in West Melton. An observatory official guides our eyes to the constellation by instructing us to focus on two bright pointer stars. The outermost of these is Alpha Centauri, which is invisible from much of the Northern Hemisphere, including all of Canada. Along with other Scouting families, Vilis, the boys, and I huddle in the cold darkness and soak up information about the Southern Cross and its pointers while waiting to gaze through a telescope.

Alpha Centauri, we're told, is a not one star but three: a binary yellow-orange star 4.4 light years away (Alpha Centauri A and Alpha Centauri B) plus a red dwarf 4.2 light years away. The red dwarf is Proxima Centauri, our nearest stellar neighbour beyond Sol, our sun. When I look through the telescope, Alpha Centauri is revealed as a smudged ball of light. Here in New Zealand, this star system, which for me has been a mystery-shrouded name in textbooks and science fiction novels, becomes real.

September 29

IN CANTERBURY Museum in downtown Christchurch, a moa-hunter creeps toward a chunky, heavy-set bird that towers above him. Both models are frozen in time and space. Smaller native birds also stand motionless, recreated by taxidermists for this diorama. Dainis, Jānis, and I marvel at the size of the giant moa (with emu feathers substituting for the real thing) and at nearby displays of woven mats, baskets (*kete*), capes, and shelters created by Māori hands. We study bone fishhooks and gleaming jade clubs (*mere*), bats (*patu*), and earrings and pendants. The weapons, household goods, and ornaments make the lives of New Zealand's early inhabitants suddenly seem more real to us.

After leaving the museum, we wander through the adjacent Christchurch Botanic Gardens, where ducks waddle across lawns or rest in the shade of an intoxicating variety of specimen trees: cypress, palm, redwood, eucalyptus, red beech, oak, maple, and many more. Tree ferns fling curved fronds to the sky, and armies of tulips bear brilliant torches of colour. A few rhododendrons among the masses planted within the gardens bear clusters of translucent flowers in the soft, sweet shades of old-fashioned, spring prom dresses.

We explore more of downtown Christchurch and pause at the Boulevard Bakery Café to sample steak and mushroom pies, which are delicious. I note donuts on the dessert menu, and we each order one, only to receive a surprise on their arrival.

"They're not *real* donuts," Jānis grumbles quietly.

"Yeah. They're just bread with some icing on it," Dainis mutters.

I commiserate with the boys while we munch our way through the plain, sturdy New Zealand donuts. Like several other Kiwi foods (examples being the bland tomato sauce that substitutes for ketchup and the hotdogs that turned out to be sausages on sticks) these donuts just don't satisfy our Canadian taste buds, in this case, accustomed to the soft, sugar-dusted donut variety, not to mention the intoxicating assortment available at Tim Hortons. On the other hand, New Zealand's hard ice cream flavours are among the best we've ever tasted. There's nothing like a cone piled high with Hokey Pokey (vanilla ice cream imbedded with nuggets of sponge toffee) to celebrate completion of an outdoor adventure.

September 30

PŪKEKO BOB their heads as they stride across a mudflat beside Brooklands Lagoon, a coastal, brackish wetland near the mouth of Waimakariri River, fifteen kilometres north of Christchurch. Black-backed gulls fly over the lagoon or stand near its edge. Their dramatic black and white plumage contrasts with the beige-russet of old reeds and grasses growing along the wetland's shores.

NEW ZEALAND FLAX AT BROOKLANDS LAGOON

This morning, our chosen track is a section of Waimakariri Walkway on Brooklands Spit, a narrow strip of sand dunes that separates Brooklands Lagoon from the ocean. At the trailhead, creaking, wind-nudged trees suggest grey ghosts squeaking out whispered greetings. A female chaffinch inspects us curiously.

The track leads us from the whispering trees to sand dunes covered with stiff, poky marram grass and occasional small thickets of stunted pines. Where exposed, the sand is pale beige, its muted colour relieved by magenta flowers. We flush a male blackbird from the trail and spot a fantail in a copse of pines. Redpolls chitter

IN DENSE SCRUB BESIDE BROOKLANDS LAGOON

overhead, and skylarks pour out their tinkling songs. Of the five bird species we see, only the fantail is a native New Zealand bird.

As we hike, the dunes shield us from the surf's roar and the open expanse of the lagoon. We scale a dune for a longer view, only to discover that from the new position the lagoon's water is now hidden, its surface an expanse of grassy, reddish-brown vegetation. Vilis and the boys thrash down the slope through marram grass, gorse, and robust clumps of plants having long, straplike leaves (New Zealand flax, I later learned) to an enticing mound of "sit-able" shrub and fling themselves onto it with exultant cries.

Steady rain sweeps in off the ocean. My family returns to me, and we tramp across a sand basin riddled with small holes. Tiny, mud-coloured crabs lunge partway out of holes when we step near and then withdraw into the sandy depths when our footsteps recede. Vilis reaches down to capture a crab to inspect. However, the hunting crab captures his finger instead, much to our sons' amusement.

The rain persists. We decide to cut our hike short, and scramble from the dunes onto the beach for the return hike.

ON THE BEACH AT BROOKLANDS SPIT

The beach is magnificent. Hard-packed sand stretches north and south, its surface like wet pavement leading to the Pacific's turmoil. At the ocean's edge, massive grey-green waves laced with white froth crash onto shore, their murky waters sandwiched between the roiling blues of a stormy sky and the same blues reflected by wet sand.

A half-dozen jet ski riders in wetsuits slam their machines into the waves and rocket upward. They resemble ants crawling over a battling dragon. One rider capsizes his machine and loses hold of it, then somehow retrieves it in the swirling, pounding surf. Along with his companions, he attacks the waves again and again.

Finally, I turn away from the wild ocean and thrill seekers. When I check for my family, I spot Vilis and Dainis silhouetted against brilliant reflecting sand. They look like they're walking on water.

October 2

THE SUN we ached to see during August's and September's frustrating weeks of confining rain has rapidly become a foe to respect. Today, heat pours over Lincoln, sailing through the township on strong northwest winds that hold drought in their breath. These winds, I think, must be the hedge winds – the reason for the immense, sheared hedges enclosing pastures and fields in Canterbury. Like castle walls protecting courtyards of green, the living barricades act as bastions against moving, slamming heat that sucks up moisture in soaring rates of evaporation. If this is spring, what will summer bring?

While Vilis's reading to the boys immerses them in Mona Anderson's adventures on a South Island high-country sheep station, my reading vaults my sons and me to North Island just after the turn of the twentieth century. This morning, we meet nine-year-old May Tarrant, the real-life heroine of Phyllis Johnston's *Black Boots and Buttonhooks*. The time is 1907, and the place is Paemako, only seventy-five kilometres north of the Tongariro Forest Conservation Area where my family will live-trap stoats.

That region is known as King Country because in 1858, the North Island Māori elected a king as a means to bring together their many factions, in order to withstand the onslaught of the Pākehā's colonial invasion. Their first king was Te Wherowhero, an elderly Waikato chief who led his people toward establishing a unified system of law and order that decreed that no more land in the Central North Island was to be sold to Pākehā.[80]

At the book's opening, however, it's a different story. May's English family has moved to Paemako, her father having won in a lottery the right to buy 150 acres of bush with assistance from the government's Improved Farm Scheme. A land rush is on, and settlers like May's father and brothers clear bush from their land with the hope of establishing rich dairy country that will make them wealthy.[81]

October 4

TODAY, SCHOOLING is a rocky affair. The boys are argumentative and as unsettled as New Zealand's weather. Jānis erupts into grumpiness as though his temper is linked with the hot winds that again blast Lincoln from the northwest. Our afternoon drive to the rink gives him cooling space, and tension eases from his face while he skates.

On our return drive, battling winds shake the car and shove us about on the road. The northwest wind flees before a southern blast that pours hard splats of rain across the windshield. At home, Dainis calls out that his tennis lesson has been cancelled. Jānis and I dash out the back door to collect rain-spotted laundry, half of which lies limp on the grass like scattered bits of wind-broken bodies.

October 6

AFTER TEA on another blustery day, Vilis opens several envelopes and spills stamps onto the kitchen table's dark wood.

"Where did you get them all?" Dainis asks, his eyes shining.

"Oh, I happened to mention at Landcare that my sons like to collect stamps, and pretty soon, people started bringing in envelopes of stamps."

"That was kind of them," I say, noting the happiness on my sons' faces.

Now comes an exercise in bargaining and fairness. The boys and I untangle the jumbled collage of shapes and colours until all the stamps are visible and grouped by subject. Then we identify our highest priority stamps (I also collect stamps), and Vilis officiates while we take turns choosing treasures. One of my top picks is a New Zealand forty-five cent stamp that depicts two Australian brushtail possums and a European rabbit. Its caption reads: CONTROL ANIMAL PESTS.

Later, I glue this stamp in my scrapbook beneath a photograph of Vilis in his Landcare office. After all, it was an animal pest, the stoat, that brought us here.

October 7

COLD RAIN streams from the sky in what feels like the middle of the night as we dash to the car to drive Jānis to the rink for his 6:00 a.m. skate. In the dim light, roads look like straight grey tongues stretched out to catch rain drops. Christchurch appears as a clutter of drab, walled yards and commercial buildings surrounded by too much cement and asphalt to afford any beauty.

After Jānis skates, we shop for necessities and peruse a stamp show at the Hotel Grand Chancellor. I buy several packets of bird stamps, and Dainis and Jānis delight in a quiz that has them racing from display to display to locate stamp trivia. Ten thousand pages of stamps from both sides of the Tasman Sea take their toll and by late afternoon, our minds reel.

Inclement weather and lack of friends have also taken their toll during our first two months in this country. Too often, I find myself prowling like a caged lioness, restless to explore beyond Lincoln and Christchurch. I try to deal with my adventure frustration through skating, running, and immersing myself in my sons' education. Even so, I count the days slipping by while our New Zealand travel guide rests on my desk, many pages earmarked and highlighted. Dainis and Jānis deeply miss their friends in Canada and have spent too much time indoors with just each other for company. They alternate between being best buddies and firing verbal barbs at invisible targets on each other's backs. Their volatile moods have me praying for friends and fine weather. We've learned that our days here aren't always filled with adventure and exciting new discoveries, and we've all had to step outside our comfort zone and rely on each other more than we do at home. That makes for good family bonding – and sometimes, frayed tempers.

Vilis continues to take our questions about puzzling aspects of Kiwi life to work. At tea time (also called smoko or brew, but not coffee break, even though almost everyone at Landcare drinks coffee and hardly anyone smokes) he pulls out his notebook. His colleagues smile when they see the notebook and say, "What do you have for us today, Vilis?"

Here's an example. Just days ago, Vilis and I read ads in a

Christchurch newspaper referring to body armour for sale. Why, we thought naively, would New Zealanders have suits of armour? When Vilis mentioned the ads during smoko, his colleagues chortled and explained that the armour in question is protective padding worn by mountain bikers. And so, we piece together more bits of the New Zealand lifestyle.

October 8

HAZE IS a thin veil beneath a bald sun as my family hikes through pasture at the start of Mount Bradley Walkway. Eight weeks have passed since our aborted tramp in August, so we hope the "TRACK CLOSED DUE TO LAMBING" sign has been removed. However, it remains, so again we seek another track. This time we choose Ōrongomai Track in Kennedy's Bush Reserve, one of many hiking trails in the Port Hills, accessed from Summit Road.

At Sign of the Bellbird, a triangular stile of grey wood with four steps nailed onto each of its two slanting sides entices us to climb to the top step, cross a fence, and enter a rumpled pasture. The pasture extends downhill to native bush that clings to a valley crease and creeps up a section of the Port Hills. On slopes above the bush, gorse flames with deep yellow fire, like a vanguard for a forest long ago plundered by men and now regenerating and advancing. The gorse releases its troops high on the hilltops, and grassland sweeps across the exposed crest.

In the distance, the Canterbury Plain is a hazy blur of field and hedge. At its western edge, the Southern Alps rise through the haze like dark mountain cake dripping snow icing. Vilis tugs our camera from its case. "Now that's a real New Zealand scene." He composes a portrait photograph of the stile against its backdrop.

STILE AT SIGN OF THE BELLBIRD

"There we go. Stiles of New Zealand, number three."

We hike downhill through the pasture and step onto a simple bench stile to cross a five-strand wire fence. Then we follow Ōrongomai Track through the native bush we saw earlier from our vantage point. Straight, tall *matai* – evergreen coniferous trees that produce fleshy "berries" rather than cones – push thick boles up through the tousled leaf canopies of shorter trees. (New Zealand has twenty species of conifer trees, but only a trio of these produce cones. Their seeds are wind-dispersed. The other seventeen species are members of the podocarp family. They produce fleshy, berry-like structures to attract birds to disperse their seeds.[82]) The broad *matai* trunks are mottled with lichens, tufted with clumps of drooping ferns, and blistered with blood-red scars where rounded pads of bark have recently peeled off.

A fantail dances against the forest foliage, and bellbirds (called *makomako*, *korimako*, or *titimoko* by the Māori) are green and black shadows, their voices seeming to ring the bells of heaven.

For two hours, we explore the loop track, gathering fronds of various fern species to begin a collection. We also gather ragged bark strips from shrubby *mānuka* trees and long, flat fallen leaves of cabbage trees (*tī kōuka*) to weave into baskets.

On a steep, uphill section of track, we encounter tangled deadfall caused by a recent slip (landslide). Trees litter the ravaged ground and lean crazily above it. We skirt the damaged forest and pause for a rest where the track borders a rough clearing inhabited by a weathered arboreal giant. The tree's bark is grey and lined, its massive trunk dented by a sunken fissure around which sun-gilded insects buzz in a dense cluster.

"Those look like bees," Vilis says. "I think that's a honey tree."

Through my binoculars, I observe that bees are indeed crawling into and out of the fissure. Vilis thrashes through thick groundcover to a position nearer the tree, which he photographs. The boys and I remain on the track, the excitement of suspense in our laughter. If the bees attack Vilis and he bolts for the track, we're ready to run. However, my husband returns unstung, and the four of us leave the bees to their honey tree.

ON ŌRONGOMAI TRACK

October 9

TODAY IS Canada's Thanksgiving Day holiday, and we've abandoned schooling and a half day of work to venture southwest from Lincoln toward Mount Hutt in the Southern Alps. If we were at home in

Nova Scotia, we might hike in the Cobequid Mountains today, enjoying the yellow, orange, and red autumn foliage of sugar maple trees before tucking into a feast of roast chicken with cranberry sauce, mashed potatoes, other garden vegetables, and a dessert of pumpkin pie with whipped cream – all in celebration of the harvest. But we're here in New Zealand where there's no official Thanksgiving Day, so we're heading to the Southern Alps for a picnic. I promised Vilis and the boys that I'd bake a pumpkin pie sometime soon.

In west Canterbury, emerald pastures speckled with sheep lie brilliant beneath blue sky, their lush colour almost painful to observe. Surprisingly uneven groves of trees ruffle the pastures' borders. Beyond those trees, hillsides darkened by tidy pine plantations mound upward at the feet of soaring, snow-dusted mountains.

WEST CANTERBURY

The pavement leads us through prime Canterbury grazing land to the banks of the broad, braided Rakaia River. To the west of the bridge, turbid water pushes grey and fast between vertical, tree-clad rock walls that loom black beneath the sun. The gap between those walls is Rakaia Gorge, gateway to the high country and Mona Anderson's world. Only thirty kilometres west of Rakaia Gorge, Anderson's mighty Wilberforce River dumps its guts of silt and stones into the Rakaia. Here, between the gorge and bridge, the riverbed widens into a broad belly of grey stones. The rushing water splits into two courses that pass beneath the bridge, and then into many more as the river begins its traverse of the Canterbury Plain en route to the Pacific Ocean.

From the bridge, we drive south into forested foothills and turn onto Mount Hutt Road, keen to see the view from Mount Hutt Ski Area. The gravel road is coarse, dauntingly steep, and has no guardrails. I shrink away from sheer drop-offs while the station wagon labours upward. "I don't know if the car can make it up here," Vilis muses, his gaze intent on the road. "There was a mountain bike trail lower down. Maybe we should hike that instead."

He manages to turn the Bomb around and parks at the roadside next to the track. We hike through native bush and then out onto an open hilltop, yellow with gorse. The boys slash at the prickly invasive shrubs with stick-swords they found in the woods. In the distance, the Canterbury Plain spreads a verdant backdrop of fields and pastures far and wide. When our sons withdraw their attack, we strike out down the trail into the bush.

"What's that noise?" I ask, aware of a faint rumble.

"*Move!*" Vilis yells, and we leap off the track.

An instant later, a startling figure careers down the hillside, his mountain bike springboarding off bumps. His head and body are covered in black, as though he's some aberrant knight seeking prey to slay. He flashes past us and skids around a corner, in complete control.

The boys rave about the rider's skill.

"Did you notice that he was wearing body armour?" Vilis asks excitedly.

Hence the warriorlike appearance.

The remainder of our hike is tame; however, as we drive down the road later, we pass a parked vehicle and a man removing dark protection from his body. He looks up and, with recognition on his face, flashes us a conspiratorial smile.

THE LONG drive home sparks Dainis and Jānis into restless sniping. To relieve the tedium, Vilis suggests a word game wherein each of us must name an animal whose name begins with the last letter of the previous animal. *Ant. Tiger. Rhinoceros. Sunfish. Hippopotamus...* As the kilometres fly by, I realize the depth of zoological knowledge my sons have absorbed through reading and growing up with two biologists as parents. Our mealtime conversations often include biological anecdotes, the boys' favourites being the gory ones.

The game entertains us for a half hour, but at last, Dainis appears to be stumped. His alphabetical-zoological task is to conjure up yet another critter whose name begins with *e*.

I gaze out the car window at sheep pastures, at cattle pastures, and then at a paddock of ostriches. "Look, there's an ostrich!" I point out to the boys.

"Emu," Dainis tells me.

"No, it's an ostrich," I say.

"Emu," he repeats more firmly.

"*Ostrich*," Jānis corrects.

"It's my *word*," Dainis explains with a quick grin. "My word is 'emu.' The ostrich made me think of it."

Laughter erupts, and kilometres slide past.

October 10

IN THE darkness of 4:50 a.m., Vilis and Jānis rise from their beds. A short time later, I hear the *ka-dunk*, *ka-dunk*, *ka-dunk* of Jānis's wheeled skate bag bumping down the front steps, followed by a gritty rolling sound of wheels on the cement path and gravel driveway. In the darkness before dawn, the ice calls.

Hours later, I take to the ice, too. At the conclusion of the hour-long Coffee Club lesson, one of the other skaters, Sabrina with the blond pixie cut, asks, "So, where are your children when you're at the rink?"

I quell an impulse to ask her where *her* children are when *she's* at the rink. She's likely just curious about how homeschooling works. In after-skating conversations with Coffee Clubbers, I've mentioned that my family homeschools. I answer, "My husband supervises them." I don't explain Vilis's and my teaching schedules (he takes Tuesday and Thursday mornings so I can skate; I deal with the rest) nor do I mention the fact that today is the one day when the boys are on their own while I skate.

'They'll be fine,' Vilis insisted before leaving to attend a quad-driver training course.

Upon my return home, I find that indeed, all is well. Serenity reigns.

Serenity flees during the afternoon. The boys leap into Cub and Scout projects and seek my advice at every turn. The kitchen becomes a cauldron of creativity. While Jānis adds a *mānuka* bark rim to the cabbage tree leaf basket he wove during the past two evenings, Dainis plans and prepares a three-course supper as a requirement for a Scout badge.

When I glance at Janis's completed basket, it seems bare. "Would you like some cookies in your basket to take to Cubs?"

His eyes light up. "I think the Cubs would love some cookies."

Racing against the clock, I bake chocolate chip cookies and set them on a clean tea towel within the basket, which Jānis will present as a Kiwi Project this evening. Then the dust settles.

Later, I unwind in the blessed silence of an empty house. My sense of self, earlier lost in the intense demands of assisting my children, once again surfaces. I pull on my coat and walk the streets. Cool evening air kisses my face, and a fitful breeze whispers secrets. The blue-grey sky merges with pavement to create a muted canvas spattered with the pinks and greens of a spring dusk on North Belt, Lincoln.

As I walk, it occurs to me that we're falling into a similar trap of hectic activities here as we did in Canada, though we were determined that wouldn't happen in New Zealand. Flexibility was to be our motto. And exploration. Yet, Vilis and I have sons aching for interactions with children other than a brother, and ten months is a long time in a child's life. Thus comes compromise: involving Dainis and Jānis in social events, but not allowing those events to dictate how all our time is spent. Who knows? If we learn our lesson here, perhaps we'll apply it when we return to Canada.

Back at the house, I record the day's events on the laptop. I'm determined to carve out a role for myself other than mother, teacher, and project advisor during our remaining time in this country. I desperately need something for myself, something *of* myself. I fill that need as I piece together words describing not only today's experiences, but earlier ones, too. It's as though a floodgate has opened, and a book is being born.

October 11

TODAY IS the day from hell as far as Jānis and his mathematics lesson are concerned. He runs from the kitchen in tears, shouting, "I hate New Zealand!" The boys' bedroom door slams closed.

"What does New Zealand have to do with math?" Dainis asks calmly.

Perhaps it's a dream shattered. Perhaps Jānis's vision of adventures in a strange land has been reduced to the loneliness of having only his family for company, the emotional pain of overwhelming homesickness, and the knowledge that every morning he must face his educational nemesis: mathematics. As the lone student in his class, he has no classmates struggling with the same concepts he battles. He has only Dainis, his older brother who methodically works his way through more advanced assignments. On top of that, Jānis sets incredibly high standards for himself, as does Dainis. And for both, the fact that their parents are their teachers eliminates an avenue of complaint about assignments that's available to non-homeschooled students.

What to do? I'm unsure how to deal with my younger son's schoolwork frustrations other than to offer patient instruction and encouragement and to push for as many outdoor excursions as possible. It was Jānis who leapt at the chance to travel to New Zealand, which he now professes to hate. Dainis had reservations, yet he's adapting quite easily to life in Lincoln. He pursues his studies with quiet diligence and the occasional dryly sarcastic comment, just as he did at home in Nova Scotia. A fifth of our time in this country has passed. What insights will the remaining months bring?

My stomach knots. I want to cradle Jānis in my arms, to tell him that I know he's lonely and misses home. That sometimes *I'm* lonely and miss home, too, no matter how many adventures the four of us have here. There's a place, a place so deeply entrenched within us, that when we're away from it, we feel adrift. That place is home, Ravenhill. And we're here, not there. So Jānis is adrift – painfully adrift – and occasionally, he crashes into rocky shores, particularly during math lessons. I knock on his bedroom door. "Jāni?"

IN LATE afternoon, after returning from the rink with Jānis, I ask Dainis, "How did your lesson go?" Today he met his tennis coach for the first time.

My older son's entire body radiates disappointment. He grumbles, "She told me I have to change my serve, and we spent nearly all the time practicing serves, forehands, and backhands. We hardly had any time to play games."

In a day already fractured by tensions, Dainis's much-anticipated lessons have collided with another reality.

October 12

ELLESMERE ROAD is strewn with sodden leaves and flower petals – confetti tossed in a violent marriage of air and water. Cattle and sheep huddle in pasture corners, their heads lowered, their rumps to the wailing wind as the deluge of rain slants down onto Canterbury. In Christchurch, traffic crawls and is lighter than usual for a Thursday morning. No doubt, many Cantabrians are of the same opinion as Jānis, who on seeing windows lashed with rain driven by a gale-force wind, said, "This is some day. It's a day to do indoor chores."

At the rink, benches beside the ice are empty. Rain on the roof beats a drum roll that increases and decreases in amplitude. I wonder if I'll be the lone Coffee Club skater this morning, until three others arrive.

"I saw the cars and wondered who else was daft enough to come," Danielle comments.

"Is this weather typical of spring here?" I ask.

"No!" Daphne responds. "This is more like Auckland weather, or maybe Wellington's."

"It's a winter storm," Danielle explains. "We didn't really even have winter this year. And we've had so much rain already. Christchurch is usually so dry."

Daphne bemoans the fate of her fruit trees in the storm, and coach Chris Street tells of someone who had to saw up a windfall to remove it from his driveway.

Then we're skating, and for much of the hour, I'm joyfully oblivious to the storm. Nothing exists except the ice, my feet, and my mind completely focused on telegraphing to my muscles the movements necessary for pumping and slalom and sculling, for clean stroking, for progressives and chassés, and for inside and outside edges. Only once am I startled out of my concentration by a thunderous unleashing of rain onto the roof.

"So, how are you going? All right then?" asks Danielle.

"I'm enjoying it," I reply while unlacing my skates. "It's coming along,"

"Feeling a bit more confident?"

"Yes."

When I exit the rink, I notice water dripping into a red bucket from a leak in the foyer roof. Outside, rain pelts down even harder than when I arrived. Pools of water have accumulated in low spots on the streets, and a wild wind blows sheets of rain horizontally, so strong they rock the car when I stop for a red light. Outside the city, water spreads across fields and pastures. The sheep in one paddock graze on both sides of what's fast becoming a lake. I drive cautiously, the wind dead against me on the last stretch toward Lincoln. The station wagon's windshield wipers barely clear the rain.

"That small tree in the yard fell down," Jānis tells me after I dash from the garage into the house. He shows me a lilac broken at the base, many of its white blossoms severed and lying limp on the lawn.

The house creaks and groans during the afternoon. Wind sifts through back door cracks, repeatedly teasing the two squeaky kitchen doors open and closed until I snap their catches securely in place. I look out a kitchen window at the tree branches' mad dance and agree with Jānis that yes, this is a day to do indoor chores.

When Vilis – who got drenched cycling to the grocery store at lunch time, then took the car back to Landcare – arrives home, he tells us of a tree blown down at Landcare, a glass entrance door shattered when the wind caught and slammed it open, and of greenhouse workers sent home because glass was breaking all around them.

We listen in awe to a radio report listing the havoc wreaked by the storm: Christchurch traffic lights blown around the wrong way by 95-kilometre-per-hour winds, hundreds of city trees fallen across roads and rivers, residents evacuated from flooded Sumner, a dozen yachts sunk at the marina in Lyttelton Harbour due to hurricane-force winds lashing Banks Peninsula.

I picture the serenity of the marina when we tramped a hillside above it a month ago and then try to envision the wreckage described in the radio report. In her prologue to *The Bone People*, New Zealand novelist Keri Hulme wrote, "In the beginning, it was darkness, and more fear, and a howling wind across the sea."[83] That smacks of Canterbury today.

After a hurried meal of pizza, Dainis is halfway into his Scout uniform when Scout leader Dave Lord knocks on our door. Tanned and rugged, he tells us that the Scout meeting is cancelled. "There are so many trees down on the roads that most of the Scouts can't get into Lincoln," he explains.

After Dave leaves, Dainis heaves a sigh heavy with disappointment and slowly removes his uniform shirt. Vilis and I convince him to come for a family walk, and the four of us stroll through our neighbourhood. Streets stretch empty, their gutters cluttered with storm-thrown leaves and flowers. Warily, we eye the huge oaks in Liffey Reserve and the slim, tall eucalypts down the street from our house. Even these giants are at the mercy of the wind.

October 13

SUNSHINE WARMS my back and shoulders while I trowel weeds from a triangular patch of soil on the northeast side of the bungalow, intending to plant bean seeds I bought at Hammer Hardware. The gardener in me has to plant something. A light afternoon breeze rustles shrub leaves behind me, and in a neighbour's yard, a lawnmower's dull roar is a comfortingly ordinary sound. Few people, enjoying this afternoon's bright serenity, would believe that at the same time yesterday, the worst storm in a decade held central Canterbury in its grip.[84]

'This place has the most changeable weather of anywhere I've lived,' Vilis muttered while dressing this morning.

Slender and exposed in a huge southern ocean, New Zealand is a country with no geographic location more than 130 kilometres from the ocean and its warring pressure systems.[85] When Kiwis talk about the weather, they always do so in terms of the winds: the northwesterlies, the easterlies, the southerlies. We've experienced several days of the strong, warm northwesterlies that characterize Canterbury in summer. Yesterday was a dramatic example of what a fierce, cold southerly brings. We've yet to experience the cool easterlies that apparently rob summer days of their heat.

I add piles of excavated weeds to a compost heap and bring in laundry while Dainis completes chores. In the boys' bedroom, Jānis naps, worn out by his schooling battles this week. His blond head rests on a pillowcase patterned with brightly coloured parrots, one of three Ps he yearns to see in this country: parrots, penguins, and palm trees.

I've researched the first P and know that New Zealand is home to three native parrots, the *kea*, *kākā*, and *kākāpō*, and three native parakeets, the yellow- and red-crowned parakeets (both *kākāriki* in Māori) and Antipodes Island parakeet. Four Australian parrots, the sulphur-crested cockatoo, galah, crimson rosella, and eastern rosella, were introduced, mainly to North Island.

Considering New Zealand's proximity to Antarctica, it's not surprising that the country is well-endowed with the second P, penguins. Thirteen penguin species, ranging in size from the world's smallest, the blue penguin, to the huge emperor penguin, frequent this country's coasts.

As far as native palm trees go, there's only one, the *nīkau*. In eastern Canterbury's agricultural landscape, our best bet for finding *nīkau* is Nīkau Palm Gully on Banks Peninsula, a destination I've earmarked for future exploration.

Perhaps muted by yesterday's storm, today is a quiet, ephemeral interlude brightened by pleasant sunshine and several vividly coloured acrylic paintings that lie like decorations on our kitchen table. This morning, Dainis painted the view through the kitchen window – all luscious greens and bright blues, with a smear of pink representing azalea blossoms thrown down onto the lawn by yesterday's storm; everything bordered in a frame of brilliant red. Jānis painted a house of magenta-rust bricks set against rounded brown hills, and then came up with the idea of painting fireworks onto black paper. I concocted a Port Hills-y work of cabbage trees set against dry hills and greenish-blue ocean. When I mixed the blue, white, and green paints to create the desired hue for the ocean, a sudden swirl of white on blue had me envisioning the surf pounding onto the beach at Brooklands Spit two weeks ago, so I painted that, too. It was like play, and there was no right or wrong, not even any answer. The only caveat was not to go too far, not to add more brushstrokes than needed, for in art, as in life, I've found that less is often better than more.

October 14

A ROAD sign's blunt message: YOU'RE A LONG TIME DEAD, SO WHAT'S THE HURRY? bears down on us and then sweeps away, leaving only open highway. Intent on tramping in the foothills of the Southern Alps, we drive south through sheep and cattle pastures and past pine plantations marred by blow downs, perhaps the result of the recent storm. In the distance, the Southern Alps – Canterbury's sharply protruding western bones – rear up against clear blue sky. Five days ago, those mountains captivated us. Today, we seek another sip from their bucket of exhilarating promise.

Forty kilometres east of Rakaia Gorge, the Rakaia River forms a vast expanse of interlacing stone and water more than two kilometres wide. We cross it on New Zealand's longest bridge and pass the town of Rakaia before angling southwest toward Mount Somers, a low peak twenty-five kilometres south of Mount Hutt. The boys chuckle at a motley collection of a hundred or more shoes hanging on a pasture fence and giggle at a herd of curious beef cattle crowding the same fence farther down the road. We stop to inspect the cattle. They stare, so we stare back. They crowd even closer to the fence, and Dainis and Jānis burst out laughing.

SHEEP NEAR COALMINERS FLAT

As we approach our destination of Woolshed Creek and the Coalminers Flat tracks near Mount Somers, it's obvious that spring in the foothills lags behind that in Lincoln. Lambs are small, and pastures are muted shades of brownish green.

Alongside a gravel road, stacks of beehives punctuate thick stands of Scotch broom. Gorse grows rampant over hillsides. One long slope of it is dead from herbicide spraying that left a thousand spiky grey skeletons and the spectre of ecological death in its wake. I stare at it in near-disbelief. Never before have I seen such full-scale poisoning of every living plant over such a large area. Undoubtedly, the poisoning was an attempt to rid the hillside of the highly invasive gorse, but the sheer magnitude of it shocks me to my core.

At Coalminers Flat, interpretive displays inform us that coal was discovered in the neighbouring hills in 1856 and mined between 1864 and 1968. We stroll Black Beech Walk beside Woolshed Creek, where sunlight sprays through the beeches' lacy canopy. The spindly trees stand like straight or angled poles, their black colour derived from honeydew fungus. Bees hover, lured by bright drops of liquid that hang from hair-like structures protruding through the fungus.

"The bees aren't very hostile," I say. "Maybe there's enough sweetness around…"

"That they all get drunk!" Jānis sniggers.

The bees certainly look content. And oblivious.

Woolshed Creek is bone dry, no more than a bed of grey stones edged with silver-leaved shrubs and backed by steep hills covered with beech forest. The boys clamber onto a battered, rusted coal car overturned beside the track, and we inspect remnants of a tramway and another coal car warped and torn by an unplanned plunge down a hill.

Where the path intersects Miners Track, we tramp uphill,

following the path miners walked during the Great Depression. After bankruptcy closed the mine, the miners formed a co-operative and bought it. They rode the train from the village of Mount Somers and climbed this twisting track to Blackburn Mine. They weren't allowed to walk the Jig Line, a straight, steep incline on which boxcars loaded with coal descended the hill.[86] After seeing the crumpled remains of runaway cars, we understand why.

JĀNIS AND DAINIS ON AN OVERTURNED COAL CAR

BLACKBURN MINE

Interpretive displays inform us that the mine produced a hundred tons of coal a day to fuel steam engines, and that a fire destroyed Blackburn No. 1. When a replacement mine to the north petered out, bulldozers strip-mined the coal seam and trucks hauled out coal. Every morning when the miners arrived, they were greeted by a fire in the coal seam, the lingering residue of the mine fire. Every morning, they quenched the flames and bulldozed their black gold. Then, in the night, the slumbering fire flared to life again. All this we learn from the interpretive displays.

The mine's reconstructed entrance is a black square in a dry, mounded hill. A sign: BLACKBURN MINING CO., announces its identity. Within a short length of tunnel behind the entrance we inspect spades and picks, carts, rail tracks, and other miscellaneous mining equipment.

BLACKBURN MINE

We leave the mine and explore the hilltop, its hollows cluttered with blooming gorse, its sparse grass not yet green. To the west, the summit drops into a deep valley. Beyond the valley, precipitous hills rise to a plateau backed by distant brown mountains.

Rabbit droppings litter the ground at our feet. Around us, gorse shrubs have been rabbit-pruned all the way back to their thick central stalks. The neatly clipped bushes look like thorny, chlorophyllous mushrooms. Here, plant and animal invaders are locked in a battle for survival in this marginal territory. The gorse clings to thin soil and, in turn, provides poor food for the rabbits.

My family's explorations are slow and easy, since Vilis is the only healthy one among us. I limp on a sore foot, and the boys are fighting head-clogging colds. Jānis also has a sick stomach. We pause often to drink in long views and exclaim how good it is to look out over a vast panorama and not see a single sheep. New Zealand is home to 40 million[87] of the woolly, bleating beasts and just under 4 million people.[88] This yields a ratio of at least ten sheep for every human in the land, so it's hard to get away from them. Twenty years ago, the sheep tally was even higher, at 70 million.[89] However, markets for lamb declined drastically after Great Britain joined the European Economic Community and in many ways abandoned its far-flung, former colony.[90]

We quit the hilltop and scramble down the steep Jig Line to the track beside Woolshed Creek, which we follow into an ancient silver beech forest. Dark honeydew fungus and pale lichen mottle the beeches' trunks.

Jānis thumbs at the forest. "It must be *really* old. It's black and white."

Dainis smiles. "Jānis must be feeling a little better now. He's making jokes."

"Well, I don't know," Vilis teases. "They're pretty poor jokes. Enough to make *my* stomach turn."

Homeward bound, we pause for ice cream cones in Rakaia, the "Salmon Capital of New Zealand," with its twelve-metre fibreglass salmon rising into the sky. After a study of the enticing display of hard ice cream flavours, Dainis chooses Goody-goody Gumdrops, Vilis selects Rum and Raisin, I pick Gold Rush, and Jānis opts for Boysenberry.

After the cones are eaten, we again play word games to kill time on the long drive home. First, we play the clues game, wherein we take turns providing three clues to the identity of a plant or animal. Those of us not providing clues are allowed to gain more information by asking questions, which can only be answered with yes or no or "please rephrase your question." We soon discover that Vilis's clues always include a size reference to a breadbox – "I'm smaller than a breadbox" or "I'm bigger than a breadbox" or "I'm about the size of a breadbox." Some of the mystery organisms are quickly identified with long shot guesses, while others come to light only after tortuous, minute-gobbling struggles to remember which clues have already been provided and what other useful questions could possibly be asked. The answers range from strawberries to tarantulas, from poison dart frogs to flying squirrels, with the most obscure correct response being Vilis's sister, Astra.

When we tire of clues, we jump into a rhyming game, taking turns supplying related rhyming phrases.

"I saw a stoat."

"With a big fur coat."

"In a boat."

"Going round a moat."

"I saw something over by the root."

"It sounded like a great big poot."

"Or a toot."

"Or a fart, to boot."

The boys howl with laughter.

October 19

AT THE end of Coffee Club skating, Sabrina asks, "So, what's your impression of Kiwis?"

Sabrina is the skater who asked me where my kids are when I'm at the rink. We chat frequently on and off the ice. I think she's adopted me, which is fun. "Do you mean the birds, the people, the coins, or the fruit?" I toss back while unlacing my skates.

She smiles. "Oh."

"The people? I find most are friendly and helpful."

"Good." She nods and then adds, "Until about twenty-five years ago, the fruit wasn't called kiwifruit. We called them Chinese gooseberries. It's only in the last two or three years that I've started calling them kiwifruit."

In Zamboni's, Sabrina, I, and the other Coffee Club skaters nibble at pieces of cake and sip mugs of hot chocolate topped with whipped milk and a strawberry marshmallow, the after-skating treat that accompanies Coffee Club. Conversation flows around and envelopes me. The boys and Vilis have their gateways to the New Zealand lifestyle: Cubs and Scouts, tennis, Landcare…

Coffee Club is mine.

October 20

ONCE AGAIN, Mount Hutt Road is a nightmare clinging to the torso of the mountain. Every vehicle we meet en route to Mount Hutt Ski Area forces Vilis to drive closer to the edge. I glance fearfully down sheer drop-offs and wonder how bad learning to ski can be compared with this. I half hope that maybe the car won't make it to the top…but it does.

The main ski field is a glaring white platter tipped on its side. Its skyward rim is chipped and broken, and its concave surface is lumpy and uneven. Far below, steep-sided grey hills meander down to the Canterbury Plain. The mountain air beneath clear skies is much warmer than expected, so Vilis, the boys, and I peel off layers of clothing before taking to the beginners' slope at 9:00 a.m. with our rented skis and heavy ski boots.

After experimenting on our own, we join three other beginners for an extended lesson of two-and-a-half hours. Our black-haired instructor, Bart, has the deep tan of someone who spends many hours in the sun. He unselfconsciously wears a pink pile jacket embroidered with the name "Sherry" and is extremely proficient at remembering names: "Kelly from Wellington. Grace from Melbourne. Joe from the United Kingdom. Vilis, Magi, Dainis, and Jānis from Canada."

"So, who's going to win the game?" he asks.

"Wellington," Kelly replies. "That's what we're here for – the footy."

Ah, yes. Footy. Rugby. New Zealand's national sport. This weekend, the Canterbury Crusaders host the Wellington XV in the national championship final.

Bart introduces us to tow rope etiquette, parallel stance, weight transfer and turning, stopping, and slalom. Repeatedly, we grip the rope to ascend the beginners' slope and then sweep down the snow in wide curves. *Bend knees. Transfer weight. Look in the direction you want to turn. Snowplough.* Lesson over.

KEA AT MOUNT HUTT SKI AREA

While we eat our sandwiches in the car, we score our first *P* when we observe four *kea* attacking an unattended daypack in the Mount Hutt Ski Area parking lot. The chunky parrots, which occur only in New Zealand and are the world's only alpine parrots, vigorously tug items from the daypack and tear some to shreds. One *kea* wears a silver metal band on its leg, and all have bronze belly feathers, iridescent green back feathers, and beaks like gleaming, black-tipped sickles. I wonder what the *kea* eat in this landscape of rock and snow when skiers' lunches aren't available.

Ready to tackle the higher slopes, we reapply sunscreen and venture upward. Old sports injuries to my knees and an ankle limit me to a half-dozen runs on the second slope. Vilis, Dainis, and Jānis ride the T-bar to the upper slopes again and again. They repeatedly sweep down the glaring white ski field, snowplough to its base, and rejoin the queue for the lift. I cool my heels until they make their final runs in late afternoon, then wince at the degree of sunburn on the boys' faces. Lost in the excitement of mastering the slopes, they all forgot about the intensity of the snow-reflected sunlight.

Jānis sleeps most of the way home, resting his red, irritated eyes. Foolishly, none of us wore sunglasses on the slopes. Vilis, Dainis, and I normally wear glasses, which apparently offered us some protection from the sun's glare. Jānis, poor kid, had nothing.

On our return to Lincoln, Jānis's eye discomfort intensifies, and the evening hours bring him the excruciating pain associated with snow blindness. He cries out and squeezes his eyes shut, seeking only darkness. Vilis and I apply cold compresses to his eyes and to his face, which is breaking out in blisters, until he's able to sleep. When he wakes in pain, I sit with him until the Tylenol I give him kicks in just before midnight.

October 21

THIS MORNING, I don't hear the usual *ka-dunk, ka-dunk, ka-dunk* on the steps before dawn. Jānis's eyes hurt so much, he can't open them. This means he may have to withdraw from a figure skating competition to be held in Christchurch tomorrow. Vilis gives him more Tylenol, and while the boys sleep, I take the opportunity to stroll along Gerald Street, enjoying blossoming rhododendrons beneath an overcast sky.

After returning to the house, I transplant bedding plants of cherry tomatoes, cabbages, broccolis, and spring onions, purchased at the hardware store, into a small garden bed on the north side of the bungalow. The soil is dark grey and moderately friable when damp, but light grey, hard, and nearly impossible to break into smaller pieces when dry. "Gumbo" is what my prairie-dwelling mother would call it. It possesses little organic matter, yet doesn't have the sticky feel of heavy clay.

Although the soil offers a less than auspicious start for the vegetables, I plant them as a promise, an act of bonding with this country, and as a thread of continuity with my home in Nova Scotia, where my yard holds flower, vegetable, and fruit gardens. Gardening is as much a part of me as are birding and writing. I, like my mother, have an instinctive need to work the soil, to produce food and to create living beauty with flowers.

When the boys stir, I lure them out of bed with French toast and sunglasses for Jānis, who with the aid of the shades is able to see well enough to eat. Dainis's skin is breaking out in blisters, and his and my lips, in huge cold sores. Vilis and I place cold compresses over both our sons' faces to soothe their injured skin. Otherwise, we putter, subdued by the sun's damage. Jānis glues together parts of a balsa Spitfire airplane model. Dainis makes a plaster cast of an apple.

In mid-afternoon, Vilis drives Jānis, equipped with sunglasses, to the rink so our son can practice his elements for the competition. By evening, however, Jānis is in agony again. He slumps over the kitchen table and covers his eyes with his hands.

I suggest, "Jāni, maybe you should withdraw from the competition."

He shakes his head. "I *have* to skate tomorrow. *I have to skate!*"

Vilis and I apply more compresses and once more give Jānis Tylenol to ease the inflammation and pain. Then I suggest we play a round of bridge. Jānis dons his shades again, and the atmosphere around the kitchen table escalates to ridiculous levels of giddiness as the game progresses. Both sons crash into bed with astounding cheerfulness.

October 22

VILIS MURMURS, "He looks like he's really mad. All that red."

The rawness of Jānis's sunburned face and eyes contrasts starkly with his creamy satin costume shirt and green velvet pants. Still not fully recovered, he performs his free skate program well, without the shades.

After the competition, which ran like clockwork but featured disappointingly few jumps in many skaters' programs, the three of us drive home and stumble into the house, exhausted. Dainis joins us after spending the afternoon with Josh Peters, the son of Lincoln Baptist Church's Senior Pastor, Kim Peters. I finally bake the pumpkin pie I promised Vilis and the boys two weeks ago at Thanksgiving. However, the mutton and beef fat drippings I use in place of lard (unavailable at the grocery store) result in hard, brittle pastry that smells and tastes of mutton. I screw up my face in disappointment.

After one bite, Dainis asks, "May I have ice cream instead?"
None of us finish our pie.

October 23

TODAY, ON a sunny, hazy New Zealand Labour Day, Vilis and the
boys are keen to tramp. Jānis's eyes began clearing yesterday,
although his and Dainis's faces remain red and peeling. Vilis wants to
head out immediately, but I dig in my "protective-mother" heels and
insist that we avoid the heat of the day. Back and forth, my husband
and I argue. It's not often that we lock horns over an issue, but when
we do, it's hard to back down. Eventually, Vilis agrees to a mid-
afternoon start and a shorter tramp, then he and I go our separate
ways with a definite coolness between us.

Last week when schooling difficulties arose, I tried to
comfort Jānis and remove the tension between us by telling him we
were in this together. 'Yeah,' he responded, 'but we're on opposite
sides.' Now, having aligned myself in opposition to my husband, I
understand what Jānis meant.

The thought occurs to me that maybe there's a connection
between our moods and October's wildly changeable weather. One
day, we have howling winds and pouring rain, and the next we have
brilliant sunshine. One day, we have tears or arguments, and the next
we have laughter and camaraderie. In more ways than one, our
resilience in adapting to a new country is being tested.

"I have a suggestion," Vilis says before lunch, surprising us
all. "Let's go to the Antarctic Centre."

Dainis rockets up from his chair. "Yeah!"

"When?" Janis asks tensely.

"Right after lunch."

"But you wanted to go tramping," I point out.

"I know, but why don't we go to the Antarctic Centre instead?"

I accept the olive branch, and we scramble through a quick meal before driving to the International Antarctic Centre, which is located adjacent to Christchurch International Airport. The centre is a huge complex. Most of the buildings are research facilities used by international teams of scientists conducting research on the earth's most southern continent. Inside the visitor centre, we learn that 70 percent of researchers working in Antarctica pass through the International Antarctic Centre. We also learn that Antarctica is the coldest, windiest, and driest place on Earth, with a record low temperature of -89.2° Centigrade, a recorded wind speed of 352 kilometres per hour, and only five millimetres of snow per year at the South Pole.

Mesmerized, we watch the video *Icebirds*, which depicts a year in the life of Adelie penguins living in that frigid, windblown landscape dominated by ice, rock, and ocean. We peer into a tent and supply boxes used during a New Zealand geologic expedition to Antarctica in 1991–92 and smile at the box of Hubbards Fruitful Breakfast (a morning staple for us) standing beside cooking supplies in the tent. Another video takes us to McMurdo Base and describes how an overwintering crew of men and women cope with the endless night of the Antarctic winter. They rely on social get-togethers, private diaries, physical workouts, weekly telephone calls home, flowers and fresh vegetables grown in a small, artificially lit greenhouse, and the bounty of mail and fresh supplies delivered in a mid-winter airdrop.

I peruse a September newspaper clipping that has a diagram of the continent of Antarctica. In blue above Antarctica and extending beyond its boundaries, the diagram shows a massive hole in the ozone layer of the earth's atmosphere. The article predicts that the ozone-depleted expanse will shift northward to lie over New Zealand during October. That it has done so, I have no doubt as I look at Jānis's burnt and peeling face. He dons a fur-trimmed parka and nose-wiper mittens before hamming it up on a retired expedition snowmobile in front of a painted backdrop that depicts snow-covered Antarctic mountains.

We exit the visitor centre through a replica of an ice cave carved out of the tongue of a glacier by the ocean's tides and currents, the entire cave bathed in ice blue. Outdoors, we're back in Canterbury, no longer immersed in that inhospitable and compelling land at the bottom of the world. In many ways, what we saw of Antarctica reminded me of the Canadian High Arctic, where I spent two summers researching plant ecology, although Antarctica is far more hostile to plant and animal life.

"Did it make you want to go there?" I ask Vilis.

"Yes," he admits.

"Maybe on your next leave," I tease.

We both laugh, but then he says, "In that video, one of the people spending the winter said she knew it was going to be tough, but when it was over, she said she was glad she'd done it; that it was a rejuvenating experience."

Our sons insist that a golden arches supper is in order, and since Vilis and I promised them at least one New Zealand McDonald's meal, we drive to Christchurch's Hornby Mall. The boys and Vilis order Big Macs, and I choose an item on the menu that I've never seen at any other McDonald's – the Kiwiburger. My burger arrives in a yellow box decorated with small, colourful pictures. Inside the box is an eclectic collection of ingredients sandwiched in a sesame seed bun: ketchup and mustard, pickled beet and onion slices, shredded lettuce, a slice of tomato, a beef patty, melted cheese, and a fried egg. The burger is hearty and flavourful, but the combination of ingredients isn't one I'd choose again.

At the meal's end, I flip the box closed and study the small pictures and words written beneath them, which appear to be a shorthand guide to all things Kiwi:

> Kiwis love...hot pools, rugby balls, McDonald's, snapper schools, world peace, woolly fleece, Ronald and raising beasts, chilly bins, cricket wins, fast skis, golf tees, silver ferns, kauri trees, kiwiburger, love one please. McDonald's KIWIBURGER the classic NZ burger. Cos we love All Blacks, thermal daks, egg & cheese, walking tracks, beef patty, marching girls, tomato, lettuce & paua shells, gumboots, ponga shoots, floppy hats, kiwifruit, beetroot, moggy cats, cabbage trees, onions, kakapos, kia-ora's, cheerios, jandals, sandals, ketchup, Coromandels, swandris, butterflies, mustard, fishing flies, hokey pokey, Maori haka, KIWIBURGER, that's our tucker...

"A chilly bin's a cooler," I say. "What's the significance of a silver fern?"

"It's a tree fern," pipes up Jānis.

Dainis shakes his head. "No, it's the symbol of the All Blacks."

"It could be both," I tell them. "Thermal daks? Must be long underwear. A *ponga* is a tree fern, isn't it?"

Jānis nods.

"Moggy cats?" I ask.

No one knows.

"Ah, their Cheerios are shaped like *this*." Vilis points to an S-curve of reddish-brown links portrayed on the box.

"They're sausages!" To my surprise, these Cheerios are not – as we are accustomed to in Canada – tiny *O*s of toasted oat breakfast cereal made by General Mills.

"Jandals are flip-flops. I learned that at smoko," Vilis tells us.

"The Coromandels are a place on the North Island," I say. "Swandris?" The picture is of a checked shirt, the term unfamiliar. "Māori *haka*. Perhaps that's a traditional Māori event of some kind."

"Dancing, from the look of it," Dainis says.

I finish the list. "Tucker. That's food. I've read that."

Whoa. In our ten-and-a-half-month race to get to know this country, we're still a long way from the finish line – and we're two-and-a-half months in.

October 24

CLOUD AND bird songs bring peace to the morning. Again, I trowel weeds from the overgrown garden patch on the north side of the house. It's slow work. My gloved hands break clumped soil away from the plant roots and crush it into smaller lumps, and then into loose pieces of soil. We'll see how the vegetables grow in it. Already, the tomatoes and brassicas – their roots freed from the confines of small, plastic cells – look stronger and are putting out new leaves.

I temporarily abandon the garden and drive to the rink, where I discover that my skates – like Jānis's on the weekend – feel positively *light* compared with the ski boots we wore while downhill skiing at Mount Hutt. It's as though my roots, too, have been freed, and I skim over the ice with new speed and manoeuvrability.

After I return home, I tell Jānis that Kim Lewis mentioned she'll start instructing him in ice dance. He groans, as he always does when we talk about ice dance, even though he works hard at it and agrees that he's learned valuable skills from it. I say half-seriously, "Then, at the next competition, you could do dance, too."

"No way! Not with a partner!"

"What do you mean?" Vilis asks incredulously. "You danced with Annette in Nova Scotia."

"Yeah, but she was my coach. I don't want to dance with some girl I don't even know."

"Then do it alone," I suggest. "You can do solo dances."

"Yeah, alone," Jānis says with relief.

Dainis grins. "If you can't even dance with a partner for five minutes, how are you going to spend most of your life with your spouse?"

"That's right," Vilis says, giving me a hug.

After lunch, I work in the flower bed to the west of the house, clearing weeds and setting out annual dahlias that will blossom in brilliant shades of yellow and red. Amid scattered raindrops, I set out several ageratums that will add a touch of cool blue, and drooping, succulent ice plants that will produce bright pink-and-white flowers. I could just leave the weeds, I know. I could just ignore the grown-in beds. We're here for less than a year, and I need not spend precious time on these gardens. Yet, a flower garden filled with rich blossoms is a thing of rare beauty. It feeds the soul, and the rewards it brings are so much greater than the effort of maintaining it.

Like marriage. My mind is still on our after-skating conversation. You start out with new soil: just the two of you. You plant seeds: love, commitment, respect, fun. They sprout, grow, and blossom into understanding, loyalty, tenderness. You keep the weeds out. And your soul can sing.

October 25

BENEATH ITS rough grey outer layer, the bark of *Pinus radiata* (the fast-growing Californian pine species grown by Kiwi farmers to pad their retirement funds) is a smooth, beautifully grained carver's delight. Its colour is a deep, dark red, its grain almost black. When sawed, the bark litters the surface beneath it with blood-red sawdust. Chips carved off it are dark gems. The shape of a ship's hull appears in Dainis's hands while he carves at the kitchen table. In the living room, Jānis carves rough-edged beads that he plans to string on a length of monofilament to make a necklace. He'll alternate bark beads with ivory-white screw shells he collected at Corsair Bay last month.

Silence and peace pervade the house while my sons' hands carve their objets d'art. I wonder what they think of while they carve, and if they feel the smoothness and richness of the bark seeping into them. I watch them, and in a strange way, it's as though, with each stroke, my sons are carving out a place for themselves in this unfamiliar new country.

Humans have lived on these islands for only about a thousand years, yet New Zealand is now a modern, democratic country possessing all the technological gadgets and know-how of the twenty-first century. Within a single century, from the mid-1800s to mid-1900s, this country's citizens accomplished agricultural and societal advances that took four times longer in North America and twenty times longer in Europe.[91] With its compressed, accelerated history of European colonization and industrialization, the growth of New Zealand bears a strong resemblance to the rapid growth of the pine whose bark my sons are carving.

WHILE WE eat our evening meal, Vilis cautions the boys and me, "Don't use the word 'stuffed.' It's a bad word here."

"What does it mean?" Jānis inquires.

"To have sex," Dainis answers calmly. "That's what it means in Australia."

Where did he learn that?

"If you use it, people will think you have a really foul mouth," Vilis stresses. As with the fanny pack episode, he'd been shot down again on the idiomatic front line during smoko at Landcare.

October 26

EARLIER THIS morning, Radio New Zealand National reported Māori protests after government workers cut an ancient tree (claimed to be sacred), which had been damaged in the wild wind and rain storm two weeks ago. Now, at the rink, a skater – one of the many women who have so generously welcomed me – remarks dismissively, "A thousand years ago, it was probably just a seedling." Her tone becomes resentful. "How many meetings is it going to take to decide what kind of tree to plant now? And as for the health care issue…" The sound she makes is not complimentary.

I don't know what to think. Her intolerant attitude leaves me flabbergasted.

On the ice, I stroke hard and practice forward skating skills. When my toe pick catches the ice, I tumble forward, but am up and skating again quickly and confidently.

"That was really quite graceful," Chris Street calls.

I laugh and continue.

"You've worked hard today," Sabrina, my skating buddy, comments after I skate toward her at the opposite end of the rink.

"Yes. I love it. And, so have you."

While we're removing our skates, Sabrina asks, "So, is it back to school for you?"

Although it's Vilis day to teach, I say, "Yes, back to school for me." After all, I consider simply living in this country to be an educational experience.

When I enter the house, a deflating blue balloon shoots down the hallway, its path guided by its attachment to a long strand of dental floss stretched from the kitchen door to the boys' bedroom. I peer carefully around the kitchen door frame and ask Vilis, "What are you investigating?"

"Rocket propulsion."

"Yeah!" Dainis exclaims. "We're seeing whose balloon goes the farthest." He measures the distance his balloon travelled and then removes it from the floss.

Jānis tells me, "I'm going to shoot mine now. Watch this!" His purple balloon blats like a whoopee cushion as it blasts down the hallway.

October 27

DAINIS WINCES during tea. "My legs are sore from all the hills," he says, referring to last evening's Scout outing at Bottle Lake Forest Park, north of Christchurch. The Lincoln Scout Troop rode mountain bikes up and down hills and through pine plantations, gullies, and sand. "And I clonked my forehead on the top bar of the trailer when I was getting my bike out. Good thing I had my helmet on." Then he tacks on proudly, "And I learned two new New Zealand words. A 'flattie' is a flat tire, and 'buttie' is your butt."

"How did you learn those?" I ask.

"Well, Matthew's mother said she hoped she wouldn't get a flattie because she didn't have a spare, so I knew she meant flat tire. And on the way home, Matthew said his buttie was sore, and he pointed to his…" Dainis points to his rear end.

Last evening, while Dainis collected new diminutive Kiwi slang, Nancy Borrie's daughter supervised Jānis while Vilis and I attended a dinner party at the home of a senior Landcare employee. There we dipped bread and veggie sticks into a cheesy dip, enjoyed a rich casserole that featured eggplant ("aubergine" here), and learned that moggy cats are just cats or mixed-breed cats, that thermal daks are indeed thermal underwear, and that swandris are bush or hunting shirts. We also discussed birds and stoats and the fact that New Zealand flax (a robust clumping plant with straplike leaves that was formerly used to make rope) is an entirely different plant from the blue-flowering flax grown on Canadian farms for seed. At this last bit of information, Vilis and I looked at each other sheepishly. We'd heard and read about flax here (called *harakeke* or *kōrari* in Māori), but had been envisioning it as the farm crop. No wonder we hadn't seen any!

October 28

THIS MORNING, Radio New Zealand National's Saturday morning program *Country Life* is interviewing independent radio disc jockeys. One plays 60 percent New Zealand music (much is from new artists) and admits this is a tough task, yet he's adamant that playing inexperienced artists is an encouragement to others. Another disc jockey invites anyone from off the street to enter his studio and perform. He comments that the place often feels like a party. The program ends just before 8:00 a.m. with the Austin Lounge Lizards' quirky song about human gene transmission, *Shallow End of the Gene Pool.* This new data dovetails with my growing impression of Kiwis as mavericks.

After Vilis and Jānis return from the rink, we pack daypacks and head for Banks Peninsula in our third attempt to tramp Mount Bradley Walkway. Our destination is Sign of the Packhorse, a trampers' hut perched on the saddle of Kaituna Pass.

At the trailhead, we don hats and smear thick layers of sunscreen on our legs, arms, necks, ears, and faces, and lip screen on our lips. It's 10:00 a.m. as we strike out on the first section of the track, startling a skink. The small lizard sprints into a tussock clump and freezes, granting us all an excellent view of its striped body. Skylarks sing overhead, and gorse blooms on distant hillsides. We cross a fence posted with the enticing sign:

PACKHORSE

FOLLOW WHITE-TOPPED POSTS

USE TRAIL AT OWN RISK

Bounded by barbed wire, bracken, and thorny shrubs, the track leads us through cropped pasture and then narrows into a deep rut carved by hooves of countless sheep and cattle – and perhaps packhorses. Nearby pine plantations stand like companies of soldiers on greenish-brown hillsides not yet dried by summer heat.

When we hike past a young plantation, Dainis asks for a rest in the shade, since the sun is already scorching. We climb over a fence and relax in the cool dimness cast by the pines. Filtered sunlight captures fallen needles in a golden net, and soft, new needles resemble curved green fingers. In the distance, lambs bleat, so the boys climb pine trees to "*baa*" back to them. Dainis scrambles from tree to tree for five trees, and when the fifth tree bends, swings to the ground shouting, "*Wa-hoo!* This is great fun!"

After Jānis's return to terra firma, we tramp through more open pasture before entering a plantation where the track transforms into a dark tunnel. Clumps of dead gorse stand shadowed among the pines and loom over us, their spiked branches arcing out as though to capture us. They create an element of suspense. And horror.

We leave the tunnel and tramp through two more plantations: pine and fir. The wind is up and shoves at the treetops. At last, we cross a stile beside a weathered wooden gate and tramp across a rocky pasture that sweeps up to Kaituna Pass. In the distance, Sign of the Packhorse appears as a small square perched on the saddle between the thrusting bulk of Mount Bradley to the northeast and the Remarkable Dykes to the west.

SIGN OF THE PACKHORSE ON KAITUNA PASS

Three hours and forty-five minutes after starting out, we stand beside the hut. Its corrugated metal roof rests atop sturdy stone walls. A railing and fence prevent livestock from reaching the door and a stack of firewood. An axe is chained to a pole near the firewood. A tank collects rainwater. The long drop (outhouse) situated near the hut has guy wires attached to it to tether the small structure against strong winds.

Inside the hut, we explore a spacious room equipped with two worn, mismatched couches, a log burner set into what was once a double-sided fireplace, and a metal-topped table next to large windows. Wax drippings decorate empty wine bottles, used as candle-holders, on the table. A half-filled wine skin hangs beside the windows, through which we enjoy a stunning view of the Southern Alps, the crater rim, and Lyttelton Harbour. A black and white photograph from 1920 portrays the hut, graced with a china cupboard, bouquets of flowers, lace curtains, and wicker furniture. Two smaller rooms off the main room each hold a pair of bunk beds.

Dainis laughs when he reads an entry in the hut book. "I like this comment: 'Great views, the bomb hut. Smelly walk up.' "

"Yeah." Jānis nods. "It *is* the bomb hut."

" 'Good shelter for giggly girls. Fantastic showy views. Sophie,' " Dainis reads, and then exclaims, "What a jerk! Listen to this: 'Place sucked! Smelled of cow sh**. Get a heater. Get a T.V. Get a shower. Get rid of the fireplace. WHY DON'T YA GET GOOD HUT! I'd rather sleep in horses' backside. Make the tramp shorter.' "

"Why would someone like that even come on this hike?" Vilis wonders aloud.

I look over Dainis's shoulder and read aloud the next entry, " 'I wonder whether you made a donation toward some of these "required" amenities? (I doubt it.) Get a life and stay in the city where you belong. Or leave the country.' "

The wind blasts us when we exit the hut, tossing my cap into tussock-tufted pasture. Cows that approached the hut while we rested indoors stare at us curiously, then bolt and run away. We climb a nearby hill and scramble to the top of a rock outcrop beside one of the Remarkable Dykes. These are gargantuan vertical rock slabs that once acted as lava chutes and have since been exposed by erosion.[92]

Chilled by the wind, we return to the hut and strike out for the car. Lyttelton Harbour's scintillating blue gleams to the north. Jānis glances at the water and grumbles, "I'm getting tired of Lyttelton Harbour. It's everywhere we go." It's true that the Port Hills and Banks Peninsula have become our hiking backyard.

As though to distract Jānis, a ewe and two lambs spring out from tall grass on the rock-studded slope below us, their hooves fleet and nimble as they bound down the treacherous incline. The boys exclaim about the sheep's wildness and, as though suddenly infused with it, leap and race down the hillside after them.

ON A ROCK OUTCROP NEAR THE REMARKABLE DYKES

HOURS LATER, we take our seats on the main floor of the immense Christchurch Town Hall Auditorium, where we await the 8:00 p.m.

opening of a concert presented by the Christchurch Symphony Orchestra. The program features *Sorcerer's Apprentice* by Dukas, *Organ Symphony No.1* by Guilmant, and *Fantastic Symphony* by Berlioz. We're a little rested after our six-hour tramp and dressed in somewhat appropriate concert attire. I note the auditorium's bold red-and-yellow colour scheme and its jutting balconies built in a futuristic design that hints at space and exploration.

When the opening strains of *Sorcerer's Apprentice* resound within the auditorium, I smile at Jānis and Dainis. Earlier, I told them the story of the lazy apprentice who, when ordered to scrub the floor while the sorcerer was away, put a spell on a mop, commanding it to bring buckets of water to wash the floor. And then the apprentice discovered he couldn't undo the spell. Thus began his frantic efforts, which are soon echoed in the music. *Organ Symphony No.1* is a whole different story, like a boiling in soul and blood, with Martin Setchell awakening the gleaming Rieger pipe organ in an astounding performance of talent and showmanship. Then, as though recognizing the need for peace after the first two performances, the orchestra's rendition of *Fantastic Symphony* provides a graceful conclusion, with strings singing sweetly.

After the concert, I gently grasp Jānis's arm and guide him to the car. It's 10:30 p.m., many long hours after he rose before 5:00 a.m. to skate, and he's falling asleep on his feet!

October 29

THIS MORNING'S church service is unlike any other I've attended. It's run by two nervous young men. The room is set up café-style. Young women serve crackers and cheese and take orders for tea, coffee, juice, or water. We watch a home-made video about heaven, then play a game in which we try to earn points to get into heaven. Next, we see a television commercial for DB [Dominion Breweries] Draught. Even in this surprising service, I can't figure out why that's included. Nonetheless, Kim Peters steps up to the microphone and manages to link the commercial about DB (renamed "Divine Blessings") Draught with a passage from the book of Revelation, to leave those of us gathered with nuggets of inspiration.

The service ends with a bracket of songs performed by Zest, a rock band comprised of five young women who performed earlier in the service. When my family exits the community centre, we're all in a daze. Kiwis have thrown us another curve ball, blasting our preconceptions of "church" to smithereens.

DURING THE afternoon, we explore Christchurch Botanic Gardens, within which the Avon River forms a wide, curving belt of rippling light, overhung by a green drapery of willows. Laughter floats over the water as Dainis and Jānis power a paddleboat upstream and downstream. Their bare knees pump up and down in the warm air. Their hands, at first uncertain on the rudder, soon grow confident.

In the gardens, rhododendrons flame with gold, orange, crimson, pink, and white blossoms. In a damp, shady nook, tree fern fronds spread like lacy umbrellas above our heads. In the open sunshine, a sturdy date palm extends curving leaf stalks into arcs of perfect radial symmetry.

Although the gardens feature many attractive shrubs and herbaceous plants, it's the trees that captivate us. A monkey puzzle's branches hang like spiky tails. Those of a fern-leaf beech spread in a low and unbelievably wide canopy that draws us, sighing, beneath its shelter. We touch a redwood's bark and see where other hands have rubbed it. We gaze up at what is, by far, the tallest *Pinus radiata* we've seen and learn that the species' common name is Monterey pine. The boys clamber among a Monterey cypress's thick, buttressed trunks, the wood grey and fissured as though long dead.

When we spot a eucalyptus giant, Dainis and Jānis take the tape measure Vilis happens to have in his pocket and measure the tree's basal circumference a metre above the ground. Our sons look small against the trunk, their young hands stretching the tape to its full length again and again while they work their way around the tree. "Twelve metres," Dainis calls, and we convert that to a diameter of almost four metres. Vilis, who is not quite two metres tall, stands against the tree and is dwarfed by it. The single gigantic trunk, which is twisted into a loose cinnamon-and-grey spiral, rises to seven metres before flinging out pale-skinned limbs. Amid strips of hanging bark, those limbs reach another fifteen metres into the sky like beseeching arms. We pay little attention to the grey-green leaves. It's the trunk that stirs us, the trunk and those naked arms with their soft pale bark, wrinkled at the joints.

October 30

SUCCESS AT last! Today our schooling morning has only minor and sporadic outbursts of anxiety from Jānis. *The key?* One task at a time, and no list of assignments staring my nine-year-old in the face. I split his mathematics work into four different sections and alternated them with other subjects, making each section manageable.

As always, throwing in some learning on the light side helps, too. I flex my right arm and toss Jānis a questioning look as I belt out, "Oh, the muscle on the front of the – upper arm?"

He groans at my singing and covers his ears. "Biceps."

We deal with muscles in other and sometimes less-easy-to-sing-about places before he, Dainis, and I resume our study of New Zealand history. Today, we learn about the get-rich-quick scheme of

British speculator and colonial planner Edward Gibbon Wakefield, who intended to buy land cheaply from the Māori and sell it at inflated prices to wealthy Europeans.[93]

WAKEFIELD'S PLAN FOR THE CANNIBAL ISLES

Wealthy Europeans who bought land from Wakefield's New Zealand Company would need labourers to work the land, and thus England could export residents suffering hard times as a result of the Industrial Revolution.[94] However, Wakefield didn't plan to allow just any settlers to emigrate to the Cannibal Isles. Rather, he intended to screen applicants in order to reproduce an independent, model English society in New Zealand without riff-raff and with a highly structured rural class system of landowner and labourer.[95] His plan of land ownership largely excluded the Māori, whom as historian John Miller reported, Wakefield considered, "inferior."[96] Those Māori who would lose their properties to his plan would work for wages. Miller also reported Wakefield saying that chiefs would be allotted properties "intermingled with the property of the civilized and industrious whites."[97]

Next, I read to the boys of the British government's hastily implemented plan to stop Wakefield's New Zealand Company from carrying out its vision of gaining control of large tracts of land. Settlers already in New Zealand had for years implored England to do something to stop the rampant violence of the early nineteenth century. Yet, the government had held back.

However, in 1840, the British government sent naval captain William Hobson to persuade Māori chiefs to give Queen Victoria the right to buy their land. In exchange, the Māori would receive the rights and privileges of being treated as British citizens. In this way, the government intended to pull the rug out from under Wakefield and annex Aotearoa. Hobson would declare British sovereignty over North and South Islands, expanding the British Empire.[98]

Thus was drawn up the Treaty of Waitangi, which was signed by a majority of Māori chiefs on February 6, 1840. However, some chiefs signed a Māori version of the treaty that didn't exactly match the original English version, and others didn't sign at all. Some Pākehā (whites) present at the time of the signing protested that the Māori chiefs who signed didn't fully understand the terms of the treaty.[99] (As an intriguing aside, it was after these islands were invaded by pale strangers that the many and often warring tribes coined a name for themselves. "Māori," they called each other, meaning "normal."[100])

I tell the boys, "Since we've been here, I've heard on the radio several times people saying that the Māori were cheated in the Treaty of Waitangi."

"I think they *were* cheated," Jānis says.

"So do I," Dainis adds firmly.

My sons aren't the only ones to agree. Judge and legal educator F. M. (Jock) Brookfield identified the British Crown's guilt in cheating the Māori. He wrote, "The Crown's assertion of power over New Zealand is treated as revolutionary in that it took from the chiefs who signed the Treaty of Waitangi more than they ceded and took from the non-signatories (who had ceded nothing)."[101]

History is forever a tangled web with invader and invaded, conqueror and conquered. The Māori now possess the right to have their complaints of treaty unfairness heard by the Waitangi Tribunal, which was instituted in 1985.[102]

October 31

CLOUDS AND coolness mask this morning. While I sample yet another Hubbards breakfast cereal – this one Oranges of Clementine – the radio dashes out bits of news, two of which I catch while juggling conversations with Vilis and the boys. The first reports that a magnitude 5.1 earthquake (moment magnitude scale or MMS has replaced the Richter Scale) shook the Wellington area early this morning but caused no major damage. The second states that the Māori, whose population suffers from a staggering incidence of diabetes and lung cancer, are requesting preferential access to New Zealand's medical care system, relating their request to the Treaty of Waitangi. The second bit of news reminds me of the comments I heard at the rink last week and makes me wonder about the future of Māori-Pākehā relations.

During the past few weeks, I've noticed my sons' flagging interest in our history lessons. So, I put it to a vote: *Carry on, or not?* The "nots" win, and we leave this country to its past.

AT COFFEE Club skating, Sabrina wails to me, "She has us going so fast that I'm all played out!" We're practicing the timing for two beginner ice dances – the Dutch Waltz and Canasta Tango – taught by Kim Lewis, Jānis's skating coach. For me, the swing rolls are even worse than the timing, since I haven't mastered outside edges and I don't have the balance to keep one foot off the ice for six counts: one, two, three with the leg back; four, five, six with the leg swinging forward.

It's a relief to move on to ice show practice for the *Cartoon Capers* production in December. Kim leads ten women, including Sabrina and me, through steps and patterns choreographed to fit a Chipmunks' rendition of the song *Achy Breaky Heart*. I'm such a beginner, I fear I'll hold the others back, yet I want to do this.

Kim tells us to pair up for the number's opening steps, and Sabrina and I smile as we position ourselves side by side. Then we're moving. Step left. Step right. Two bubbles. "Bubbles?" I ask, confused. "Sculls," Kim explains, then leads us through the rest of the choreography. Form two lines. Skate out and curve around.

Weave lines through each other. Form a kickline. Count one, two, three, *kick!* Down the ice (amid much laughter). Back to centre. Link arms. Create pinwheel and march in a circle. It's a wild ride on the outside of the rotating line — totally exhilarating!

At the end of the practice, Kim tells us, "Just wear what you'd wear if you were going out to a bar to do some line dancing." I look at her questioningly, so she and Daphne translate for me: jeans, a western shirt tied at the waist, a cowboy hat, and a bandana.

LATER, JĀNIS drags Vilis's heavy brown leather jacket into the study and pulls it on. He's determined to be a kiwi bird for the Cub Pack's costume party this evening in celebration of Halloween, an event I've been told has only recently caught on in New Zealand.

The leather coat hangs down to Jānis's knees. I push the sleeves inside, since kiwi don't have much in the way of wings.

"I'll have to use lots of newspapers for stuffing," he says.

"Not *stuffing*," I say, alluding to Vilis's cautionary words about the foul meaning of that word in Kiwi. "You could use a pillow."

"Use a sleeping bag," Dainis calls from the kitchen.

"How can I make a beak?" Jānis asks.

"You could carve one from Styrofoam," I suggest. "Or use a paper towel cardboard tube."

"What about my head?"

"How about that old brown cloth we found? It's rough from glue, but you could fold it over on itself."

"Akela said we'd get to eat donuts from strings. Do you think they'll be *real* donuts?"

Before tea, Vilis helps with the costume's finishing touches. Then it's ready — heavy and hot with a long yellow cardboard beak attached to Jānis's head by elastics. The jacket is plumped out with a pillow. The brown fabric is draped over Jānis's head and shoulders and held in place with more elastics. Surprisingly, he does look like a lumpy brown bird with a long beak.

Vilis helps Jānis remove the costume before we eat our evening meal of rice and Akaroa cod in a creamy onion and celery sauce. The fish is mild and fresh, and we round off the meal with slices of store-bought Jaffa Cake – marbled orange, white, and chocolate cake frosted with orange icing and decorated with chocolate sprinkles, the colours coincidentally appropriate for Halloween.

After tea, Vilis accompanies costumed Jānis to the Scout Hall, and at 8:00 p.m., I stroll the two-minute walk to the hall to collect our "kiwi." On entering the building, I see Jānis romping sans costume with four other Cubs. When I call, he hastens to me with sugar crystals around his mouth and merriment in his eyes. "We did get to eat donuts from strings! *Real* donuts. And someone asked me if I was Hiwi the Kiwi!"

Ah. And Hiwi the Kiwi is the hero of a popular New Zealand children's folksong sung by Mark de Lacy, a.k.a. The Minstrel. So, Jānis has achieved a small New Zealand success as sweet as the sugar on a *real* donut.

November 1

MORNING BRINGS cloud, coolness, and news of another earthquake. This one, a magnitude 3.9 quake, again occurred in the Wellington area. In a country that experiences over 15 000 earthquakes every year (100 to 150 of which can be felt by humans), Wellington rests on a hotspot of tectonic activity called the Wellington Fault Line. Twenty-five kilometres below the city, the thin crust of the Australian Tectonic Plate rides up over the dense, massive Pacific Tectonic Plate in what geologists refer to as a subduction interface. The scraping, sliding movement of these two plates across each other creates incredible stresses on the earth's surface. As a result the crust has broken into large pieces along major fault lines like the Wellington and Wairarapa Fault Lines. New Zealand's most powerful recorded earthquake, a magnitude 8.2 quake, occurred along the Wairarapa Fault Line in 1855 and caused major damage westward in Wellington.[103] (The earthquake that devastated Christchurch in 2011 was a magnitude 6.3 quake.[104])

SUBTERRANEAN FRICTION

All of New Zealand is underlain by geologic squashing, shoving, and tearing. The huge Pacific plate forced under the Australian plate in the north sideswipes past it under South Island, building mountains in its wake. South of South Island, the Pacific plate shoves its hulking bulk atop the Australian plate and pushes westward over it. All this subterranean friction produces about fifty earth tremors per day,[105] some of which are unfelt, and some of which split open roads and break chunks off mountains.

IN THE car after Jānis's mid-afternoon skate, I depress the Bomb's clutch, only to hear a loud snap, followed by no resistance under my foot. When I exit the car and reach down for the pedal, it swings back and forth in my hand like a broken wing. I tell Jānis, "I'll call Vilis, and we'll figure something out. This is a good place for the car to break down."

Jānis grins. "It's not a good thing that the pedal broke, but if it's gonna break, this is a good place for it to break."

"Exactly." I phone Vilis from the rink, and while Jānis and I wait, he arranges for a tow to Lincoln.

A half hour later, Ashley's Tow & Taxi arrives. The driver looks like what I imagine a Kiwi farmer should look like — ruddy and weathered face, leather boots, wool socks, shorts, a wool jersey over a plaid shirt, and a baseball cap. He doesn't say much while he loads the station wagon onto a trailer behind his 4WD "ute" (Utility Vehicle).

"She won't start?" he asks.

"The clutch pedal's broken."

"Ah. Clutch. That's bad."

I look for the silver lining to the cloud. "At least it didn't happen on a busy highway."

He nods. "Yes. Saved you that embarrassment."

The trip to Lincoln is a quiet one. Our driver hunches over the steering wheel and peers into the rear-view mirrors to check on the trailer. I feel a smile surface when he takes the same short cut we always travel. "You must know all the roads," I say.

"Aw…" He shrugs modestly. "I don't know about that."

When we arrive in Lincoln, the driver manoeuvres his ute and trailer into a parking space beside McCormick Motors Lincoln. Then he drives Jānis and me to Westpac Trust down the street. I retrieve a hundred dollars and hand it to him, after which he chauffeurs my son and me home, our arrival an hour later and noticeably more expensive than usual.

My jaw muscles are in knots, and I realize it's because Vilis and I had to hire a stranger to bail us out of trouble. We're not accustomed to that. In Nova Scotia, we have two vehicles and rescue each other, or rely on friends or co-workers for emergency rides (and do the same for them). It's an entirely different thing to pay for help.

November 2

WHILE I prepare a snack of Brie on crackers after skating, Vilis tells the boys, "Okay, we're going to do some quick science. We'll need a sock and some string."

"I know where to get the string," Jānis offers.

"I don't have any clean socks," Dainis says, sounding bored.

"It doesn't matter."

The boys giggle, then collect string and a dirty black sock.

"Roll the sock into a tight ball and tie it to the string," Vilis instructs Dainis. "Now, I need someone to swing it round and round over their head."

"I'll do it!" Jānis takes the string and, standing with knees bent and legs spread, swings the sock in a circle above his head like a cowboy twirling a lasso. "*Ya-hoo!*"

"I can smell it," Dainis comments dryly.

"I want you to—"

The sock flies off the string and thuds into the door.

"Tie that sock to the string better," Vilis says.

The boys burst into laughter and retie the sock. Then Jānis spins it above his head again.

"If you were that sock spinning around, how would you feel?" Vilis asks.

"Pushed to the outside," Dainis answers.

"Yeah. Squashed to the outside," Jānis says.

"That's right. Pushed, squashed to the outside." Vilis catches the sock and holds it still. "If the person spinning the string were to suddenly let go when the sock was here, in which direction would it fly?"

Dainis swings his arm in a curve. "Over there."

"That way," Jānis points, at a smaller angle than the one Dainis indicated.

"No, it'd go over here." Dainis indicates a different destination.

"It would fly off in the direction of where it was when the

string let go," Jānis guesses.

"Let's try it," Vilis says.

While I munch my crackers, I hear the thuds of the sock hitting the living room's bare walls, interspersed with whoops of laughter.

DURING THE evening, while Dave Lord and the Lincoln Scout Troop plan a three-day, two-night camp on Mount Somers, Scout parents bustle inside and outside the hall in a work bee. This involves cleaning, painting, and making minor repairs within the cement-block building. Awash in a sea of Kiwi accents, I'm grateful to be given the straightforward task of cleaning the exterior of the windows.

When I finish and re-enter the hall, a short, stocky woman spattered with turquoise and yellow paint fires quick questions at me. For the life of me, I can't understand what she said. Even when she repeats the questions, I'm unable to fathom her meaning and turn desperately to Vilis.

"How are you going?" he translates for me. "Is there more to do outside?"

"Oh! No, it's done." *Something so simple and in English, too?* After living in this country for three months, I thought I could comprehend basic sentences spoken in my native language. Obviously, I have a long way to go to achieve Kiwi fluency.

November 3

URGENCY IS a FIRE within me. The day disappears in a tangled rush of schooling and household chores. The laundry sink overflows three times, necessitating attention I would rather bestow on my sons' education. Dainis is a trooper, completing task after task on the chore list I composed last evening. Jānis packs for a two-night Senior Cub Camp at Waipara, north of Christchurch. Then both my sons assist me with whirlwind preparations for Nova Scotian visitors who will arrive in Lincoln late this afternoon.

Faces from home so wonderfully familiar appear at our door at 5:00 p.m. – ICU nurse Betty Hodgson, her neatly-trimmed hair as black as a moonless, starless night and the antithesis of that of her environmentalist husband, Colin Stewart, whose frizzy white hair is tied back in a ponytail. Both outdoor enthusiasts, our guests will embark upon a month's exploration of New Zealand's national parks. Betty laughingly relates how Colin invited six guests home for dinner the day before she and he departed Halifax en route to New Zealand. "I told him I should throw him out of the plane over the Pacific Ocean!"

While Vilis accompanies Jānis to the Scout Hall to send him on his way to camp, I lead Betty and Colin to Liffey Reserve, where they identify birds and toss out botanical terms that flash into my recollection from studies undertaken what seems a lifetime ago.

November 4

THIS MORNING, frost is a scattering of diamonds on the earth as I run Lincoln roadsides. Flowers in walled gardens paint brilliant splashes of colour: poppies, irises, roses, foxgloves. Clear, breezy air carries the sweet serenades of skylarks, blackbirds, and goldfinches, and the crazy cackling of spur-winged plovers.

I return home just in time to see Vilis open the door on Betty sitting on the loo.

"Oh! Sorry!" he exclaims, and swings the door closed in record time.

"Maybe you should throw Vilis out over the Pacific Ocean,

too!" I call to Betty, and smile when I hear her familiar laughter.

After breakfast, Dainis heads for the tennis courts, and Vilis drives Colin and Betty to Christchurch for a few hours of sightseeing and shopping.

I soak up my peaceful interlude in the kitchen, adding to my scrapbook. Its cover is pasted with a miniature highway-sign souvenir sticker ("SHEEP NEXT 1200 KM") and a tiny royal blue New Zealand flag with a Union Jack in the upper left corner and four red, white-bordered stars representing the Southern Cross on the right half of the flag. I've filled the scrapbook with photographs and memorabilia: flattened Kiwiburger box, our skiing passes from Mount Hutt, the newspaper advertisement for the Christchurch Symphony Orchestra concert we attended last weekend. Now as I write penciled notes in the pages' margins, each photograph and bit of memorabilia is like a tug on the tablecloth of a laden table, spilling memories into my lap. I scoop them up, pour them into my pencil, and write them back into the scrapbook.

In late morning, Dainis returns from his first tennis competition. He attempts modesty but can't help glowing with pride at his victories in both singles and doubles against the team from Leeston. Soon after, Vilis and our guests return from their Christchurch excursion.

With Jānis away at Senior Cub Camp, the five of us hasten to Crater Rim Walkway northeast of Sign of the Kiwi. We hike gentle pasture slopes to the barren, rocky peak of low Mount Vernon. It seems as though all the world is at our feet: Canterbury Plain, blue harbour, big, big ocean.

On our descent, two-step stiles offer inviting step ladders from one pasture realm to another, some closely cropped and speckled with rocks; others thick with tangles of ungrazed grass.

WITH BETTY AND COLIN ON CRATER RIM WALKWAY

East of Mount Vernon, the track leads us past Rāpaki Rock, a massive grey volcanic dyke that presents a sheer, vertical face – undoubtedly a mecca for rock climbers. Beyond Rāpaki Rock, a steep, boulder-strewn incline tempts us away from Crater Rim Walkway to the summit of Witch Hill and even more spectacular views. From this vantage point, the Port Hills roll away in tawny swells, and the jagged crater rim resembles angled teeth pointed toward Lyttelton Volcano's collapsed centre and Lyttelton Harbour.

On the summit's east side, a stone seat rests near a huge boulder bearing a plaque commemorating fallen World War I soldiers. Poignancy spills from the plaque in the words of a war poem penned by English poet Rupert Brooke in 1914:

The Dead

Blow out, you bugles, over the rich dead.
There's none of these so lonely and poor of old,
But dying, has made us rarer gifts than gold.
These laid the world away, poured out the red

Sweet wine of youth, gave up the years to be
Of work and joy, and that unhoped serene,
That men call age and those who would have been
Their sons, they give their immortality.
Blow, bugles, blow, they brought us for our dearth
Holiness, lacked so long, and love, and pain.
Honour has come back, as a king, to Earth,
And paid his subjects with a royal wage,
And nobleness walks in our ways again,
And we have come into our heritage.

Rupert Brooke
Died at Lemnos. Gallipoli Expedition.

"That was a time when people still believed in honour," Betty comments. "It's a quality that seems to be sadly lacking in our world today."

" 'On the hills he loved,' " Vilis quotes gently, reading a second plaque. "Doesn't that just paint a picture for you?"

The stone seat, we read, was erected by the parents of a young soldier and dedicated to him, his friend, and "those other gallant lads whose homes were near the foot of this hill at St. Martin's." Seven young men died far from these hills, at Gallipoli and Laventie in 1915, MacDhabar Syria in 1916, Messines in 1917, and in France during 1918, according to the plaque. It was the participation of New Zealanders in World War I – their regimental badges decorated with a dumpy, long-beaked bird – that earned the soldiers the nickname of "Kiwis," a term now synonymous with this country's residents.[106]

While Dainis curls up on a sit-able shrub to rest out of the wind, I scramble around to the far side of the rock and discover a smaller plaque inscribed with many words I can't comprehend and only a few that I can. It commemorates the loss of two Māori soldiers, one who died at Gallipoli in 1915, the other in Auckland in 1916.

With wind in our faces, Vilis, Colin, Betty, and I rest on the stone memorial seat and gaze out over the hills. In my imagination, I can almost see those nine young men striding these slopes and hear their voices caught on the wind and flung over the crater rim to the ocean.

LYTTELTON HARBOUR AND LYTTELTON VOLCANO CRATER RIM
SEEN FROM WITCH HILL

The hectic activity we encounter on our descent to Crater Rim Walkway and Summit Road is in sharp contrast to the reverence implicit in the plaques. Trampers and a dirt biker string out along the track. Cyclists, runners, and motorists are sun-gilded flashes on the pavement. Small, moving splashes of colour denote climbers on Rāpaki Rock. A wedding party of laughing young men and women ambles toward the volcanic dyke (must be climbers, we decide). A cluster of sombre women wearing long skirts that hint of medieval times poses for photographs among boulders, one of the women wearing a flower wreath on her hair. Again, Canterbury has taken to the heights.

LATER, IN evening's darkness, we sit on foam pads on a grassy hillside in Lincoln's Ellesmere Country Club, craning our necks to view a night-shattering Guy Fawkes Day fireworks display presented by the local fire department. Shadowy, smoke-wrapped figures crowd the picnic area. Children wave white or pink sparklers that spit flecks of light into the dark. Firemen veiled by smoke bend over craters, their faces thrown into bright relief by a rocket's ignition. Toddlers shriek at the explosions. The entire scene evokes the impression that we've gate crashed a pagan ritual. The wind, subdued since this morning, wafts smoke and sparks toward a pond at the bottom of the slope. A fire blazes near the pond, and a firefighter gathers spent fireworks tubes and tosses them onto the flames. In the darkness above Lincoln, competing fireworks displays spatter brilliant, ephemeral shots of light against the night.

Frigid air flows down the slope, chilling us to the bone. A wailing siren calls the firemen to duty, prematurely ending the evening's festivities. I shiver and murmur, "*Brrr!* It's cold. I'm glad I'm not sleeping outside tonight." Then I recall that Colin and Betty *will* be tenting during their travels. I ask Betty, "Which direction will you and Colin head off in?"

"We'll go north," she answers quickly.

Only in the Southern Hemisphere would a Canadian escape the cold by travelling north!

November 5

BLUSTERY, CHANGEABLE winds nudge and shove me from different directions. Morning sun is bright in my eyes. With my waking image of a swift bike ride clear in my mind, I cycle as fast as I can the six kilometres to Tai Tapu, then ride hard home. In the fields all around me, introduced songbirds sing, and I hear the distinctive cackle of the spur-winged plover. I cycle up our drive and dismount, startled by unexpected stiffness and soreness in my lower back and legs. I tell Vilis about my aches.

"Well, I guess you wouldn't do very well on Summit Road," he says, chuckling.

I picture the lean, muscular cyclists on their hi-tech bikes we saw yesterday while hiking near Rāpaki Rock. "No, I don't think I would."

JĀNIS RETURNS from Senior Cub Camp at 1:00 p.m. He's a little pink, but not badly sunburnt. "That was a *great* camp!" he enthuses. "We were put into patrols so we could learn to do things like Scouts do. I cooked supper last night – sweet and sour pork." He displays his treasure map of "Peryll Island" (artfully edged by burning that got a little out of control and destroyed a finger of paper leading to the map's centre) and then asks hopefully, "Can we go to the fireworks tonight?" He missed the display in Lincoln last evening.

"We haven't decided yet," Vilis replies, but he sees the hopeful expression on our younger son's face.

I read aloud from yesterday's issue of Christchurch's *The Press*: " 'Fireworks extravaganza set to light the sky…fireworks will be set to music…will be the first New Zealand showing of new pyrotechnic effects, similar to those used at the Sydney 2000 Olympic Games.'[107] "

"We'd have to take two cars," Colin says, "since there are six of us."

"I'll stay home and soak my sore back in a hot bath," I tell him. "That leaves only five to go, and the Bomb can take all of you."

Sated with a supper of lamb chops and mash (mashed potatoes), followed by not one, but *four* desserts provided by Colin and Betty – Mississippi mud cake, lemon cheesecake, real sugary donuts, and Boysenberry ice cream – the fireworks-watching crew prepares to depart.

"Enjoy your few hours of peace and quiet, Magi," Betty calls to me.

I laugh and reply, "I will!"

November 6

AFTER THE alarm rings, Vilis and I snuggle in bed for a few more minutes and I ask my husband about the fireworks display last evening. "How was it?"

"It was good, but the music didn't work at all. It couldn't compete with the fireworks." He thinks a moment. "We had to park a long way away and walk to the beach." He smiles. "Every time Jānis saw a small explosion of fireworks – like the ones we saw people setting off on their own in Lincoln – he would ask, 'Is that it?' There must have been thousands of people on the beach, sitting in clusters on the sand. I've never seen anything like it. But it had a nice atmosphere, and there were *tingle-tangle* in the mall."

I envision Ferris wheels, carousels, and other rides – '*tingle-tangle*' in Vilis's Latvian upbringing – brightly lit in the darkness, and shadowy shapes of people on the sand, with relaxed laughter in their voices. "So, it felt like a fair."

"Yeah, it did."

After breakfast, Colin and Betty depart, heading for Arthur's Pass, to be followed by Abel Tasman National Park on the northern tip of South Island, and then North Island.

Exhaustion prowls around Jānis, its appetite fed by two late nights at Senior Cub Camp, followed by the fireworks display last evening. He exclaims over the fireworks, wails that he'll never catch up in his Cub diary, and flames with fighting spirit as he tackles memorizing *The Fighting Téméraire*, Henry John Newbolt's poem about an English ship that fought in the Battle of Trafalgar. On and on, like a candle burning its last wax, Jānis memorizes and recites until he has eight of the twelve verses down pat. Then the candle sputters, exhaustion leaps, and he crashes into bed to sleep for hours.

"He's sleep-deprived," Dainis says kindly, and it occurs to me how much my older son has matured during this time in New Zealand. He's taking on more and more responsibilities without constant urging, and sees beyond himself to the needs of others.

November 8

COLD PERVADES the house. Rain pours down beyond the windows. The boys and I confine ourselves to the kitchen with doors closed and an electric heater on. I wonder aloud where Colin and Betty are – camped en route to Abel Tasman National Park? – and silently, if there's snow on their tent. When the boys are distracted from their schoolwork because of excessive gabbing, I bring on a spate of giggles by threatening to banish Dainis to the Antarctica of the living room.

When Vilis returns from Landcare, he shows us a postcard of the Balmoral Grist Mill we received from a friend in Nova Scotia. The mill, built in 1874, is a working museum only a kilometre from our home. The photograph on the card shows snow on the ground and on the mill's roof. The boys and I sigh at the familiar sight, each of us suddenly transported home in our thoughts.

Even so, we're more content in Lincoln now than we were in early and mid-October, when the wild, wet weather and an intense spell of homesickness threw a damper over us. Now my sons seem happier, more creative, and more at home in their respective niches in Cubs and Scouts, skating and tennis, and their Sunday School classes. I feel part of my skating group, and the boys and I continue to send Vilis off to work with lifestyle and vocabulary questions. To date, his colleagues haven't led us astray — as far as we know.

After tea, Vilis tells me, "You know, this not being able to understand what someone is saying works the other way, too." A sparkle of laughter lights his eyes. "At the rink yesterday morning, I was talking to the mother of that little girl learning to skate pairs with that tall, red-haired boy. I asked her if her daughter was keen to learn to skate pairs. She just stared at me. I repeated the question. Then, I saw understanding dawn on her face." He pauses to mimic the woman's accent, " 'Ow, yuu mane *peers!*' "

Truly, our speech must seem as peculiar to Kiwis as theirs sometimes does to us.

November 9

LAST NIGHT, the Southern Cross — night-swan constellation of the Southern Hemisphere — flew white and strong. The air sliding through my open bedroom window held the promise of frost.

This morning, ice flakes sparkle on bent curves of lawn grass and on the garage's corrugated roof. A clear sheet of brilliant blue hangs above Lincoln's cabbage trees and metal-roofed houses. With trepidation, I check my gardens. Fortunately, the frost-tender tomatoes and impatiens, sheltered near the house walls, escaped damage.

I stride past Lincoln Primary and Lincoln High School and along Boundary Road as far as the golf course. In the distance, the Port Hills thrust hazy indigo peaks against the sky, a few tufts of white cloud at their summits. Around me, goldfinches and house sparrows scatter bright sound. School buses pass me; however, these are not the conspicuous yellow school buses of North America. Rather, they're charter buses that display neon green and black "SCHOOL" signs.

As I retrace my steps, I notice a high school student crossing the road ahead of me, his school uniform a dark-green sweater and short pants. Closer to the schools, I see teenage girls wearing dark-green sweaters and long, plaid skirts that sway gently when they walk. Within this forest of older pupils, clusters of younger students stand out like bright tulips, their red pile jerseys crested with "LINCOLN PRIMARY" in royal blue thread. In the brilliant sunshine, the youngsters resemble fuzzy scarlet bees buzzing around outside their hive.

KIWI! JĀNIS observed two juvenile brown kiwi on a Cub outing to Willowbank Wildlife Reserve in Christchurch two days ago. This afternoon, he tells me, "They were about this big." He positions his hands twenty-five centimetres apart, forming an oval. "And they had really long beaks. And there was an x-ray of a kiwi with an egg inside it, and the egg was almost as big as the kiwi's body!"

You have to wonder how they do it. No other bird on earth lays an egg as large as the kiwi's, relative to its body size. The North Island brown kiwi, which inhabits the Tongariro Forest Conservation Area where Vilis will conduct his research, weighs about 2 kilograms. Females of this species lay eggs that weigh over 400 grams – more than a fifth of their body weight. Little spotted kiwi invest even more resources in their eggs. The 1.25-kilogram females lay eggs that weigh a whopping 360 grams, almost 30 percent of their body weight.[108]

THE KIWI'S LOW "FURNACE" SETTING

Kiwi lay their oversized eggs in burrows they dig in the soil of native forests, pine plantations, overgrown pastures, grasslands, and even sand dunes. The eggs are incubated by males, and sometimes by females, for at least two-and-a-half months. This is an unusually long time even given the eggs' extraordinary size. Kiwi have the lowest metabolic rate in the bird world and a body temperature two to four degrees Centigrade lower than that of other birds of equivalent size. It's this low "furnace" setting that accounts for the extended incubation of kiwi eggs. For these ancient, flightless birds, the road to parenthood is a long and energetically costly one.[109] This fact makes predation on their young by stoats even more devastating than the already morbid statistics indicate.

After listening to Jānis's excited kiwi description, I throw together a vegetable side dish for tea, with an unusual ingredient, *kūmara*, the Māori sweet potato. Its yellow flesh blends in smoothly, adding a distinctive sweet taste and mealy texture. Before the arrival of James Cook and the potato, it was *kūmara* that determined the location of permanent Māori settlements, since it was a necessary staple that couldn't be grown south of Banks Peninsula.[110] When Cook gave the Māori pigs and potatoes, he gave them more than new food sources and trading materials; he gave them a new tool for their dispersal.

November 10

AGAIN, THE Port Hills etch inviting peaks against clear sky. The Southern Alps beckon with snow-capped heights that rise high above the Canterbury Plain. I'm invaded by a restlessness that I can control only until mid-morning when the boys have completed their reading, writing, and arithmetic. Then I have to break free. "Let's go to Lake Ellesmere," I suggest. "Perhaps we'll see some new birds there. And it's close. We'll be back for lunch."

"But we haven't finished all our schooling," Jānis reminds me.

"You've done everything important. Besides, we can have a class in ornithology. That's the study of birds."

The lake is everything I need and more peaceful than I imagined. Still and serene, its surface reflects the Port Hills, a few cottony clouds, scattered clumps of tall rushes near shore, and hunters' box-shaped wooden blinds built fifty metres or more out into the shallow water. My sons and I sit on an ancient weathered tree trunk, washed up onto the shore by some past storm, and gaze out over the lake. Its serenity and the sun's surprisingly gentle warmth soak into us.

In the distance, white-faced herons tilt forward on long legs as they scan the water for prey. Pied stilts fly overhead, trailing long red legs. Mallards mutter in small rafts among black swans that sail away from us, their fuzzy beige offspring at their sides. Welcome swallows skim insects from the lake surface, their wings forming dark angles that dip and rise. Each swallow's reflection in the lake is so perfect it seems that two swallows rather than one skim the surface, one from above and one from below. Like lovers, the two come together to kiss at the water's surface then gracefully curve apart before coming together again.

For an hour, we watch the birds, soothed by a skylark's song, lulled into lassitude by the ducks' gabbling. No people, houses, or roads interrupt our quiet reverie. The lake, which is neither groomed into the manicured neatness of Lincoln yards nor bounded by the trimmed hedges bordering Canterbury pastures, stretches away before us to the horizon where mirages of trees and hunters' huts dance on rippling air.

Stirred by the sun's increasing heat, we stroll through a pasture jutting into the lake. The boys whistle brightly, as though our decision to move gave sudden permission for joyful sound. I note that the black swans don't swim away when we stroll closer, as they did earlier. Near shore, two rusty-brown and blue-grey dabbling ducks with wide bills cruise past. I raise my binoculars to study their field marks and flip through my bird guide to identify them as male Australasian shovelers. Still, even with these movements that would normally be sufficient to startle wary birds into retreat, the black swans remain near.

Suddenly, I'm listening, really *listening*.

"It's your whistling," I tell the boys. "I think the swans like your whistling. Maybe they think you're a new and interesting kind of bird."

Jānis and Dainis laugh, delighted at being thought to be birds by another bird.

"Keep whistling," I say.

The boys whistle louder and brighter than ever, and in a moment of sheer magic, the swans whistle back. Interspersed with gabbling, talking sounds, the birds issue deep, breathy notes like those produced when air is blown across the top of a long bamboo tube. The magic of the moment lights my sons' eyes. They exuberantly continue their musical discussion with the resplendent black waterfowl while we walk farther out on the point so I can identify little shags perched on the tops of fence posts protruding from the lake. Like royal friends newly acquired and enjoying a novel and entertaining conversation, the black swans accompany us. They sail alongside the boys and blow their deep-toned flutes. It's as though Dainis and Jānis are providing harmony for a symphony the swans have for too long performed alone.

With no watches among us, we don't know what time it is, other than what our bellies tell us, and they say it's time for food. Reluctantly, we bid the swans farewell, turn away from the point, and slog back across the sodden pasture.

Swarms of long-legged insects flush from thick clumps of tall rushes and hang about our faces. Above us, the male skylark continues to perform his display of territorial defence. He hovers high in the air, his wings beating madly, his song pouring down to earth.

We cross from the close-cropped pasture into one less recently grazed. The tall grass tugs at our boots, and we note that the October 12th gale washed flotsam far inland, leaving a dead swan and a brown crust on the grass that reaches as far as the willow-lined perimeter. Then we follow our stomachs home, like Winnie-the-Pooh did when he and Rabbit were lost in the forest after leading Tigger there.

On North Belt, we meet Vilis. "It was so peaceful and so *big*," I tell him, trying to communicate the serenity we felt at Lake Ellesmere. "There were no houses and no roads."

He laughs. "And no cyclists zooming past or climbers scrambling."

"Exactly! And the swans whistled back to the boys." I relate our experience. Then he's on his way to Landcare, and my sons and I return home with the lake, the sun, and the swans still stirring our souls.

November 11

MISSION: FIND palm trees for desperate palm seeker.

Destination: Nīkau Palm Gully, Banks Peninsula.

After Vilis and Jānis return from the rink, we drive south on the Christchurch Akaroa Road. If we were in Nova Scotia on this Canadian Remembrance Day, the boys and Vilis (a Cub leader) would be preparing to march with the Cubs and Scouts down the main street of Tatamagouche in the Remembrance Day Parade, and we would all attend the memorial service in Sharon United Church honouring the war dead. But we're here in New Zealand, which along with Australia, honours its war dead on April 25th. (We later learned that April 25th commemorates the loss of Kiwi and Aussie soldiers at Gallipoli.)

Near Birdlings Flat, we make the right-angle turn and follow the highway beyond Lake Forsyth into the heart of Banks Peninsula. From Cooptown to Barry's Bay, the road twists, climbs, and drops like a serpent writhing in pain as it traverses the broad tongue of land between the head of Lake Forsyth and that of Akaroa Harbour. Lush vegetation edges the road, with no gorse in sight. Red and white swirling designs on rock walls create vivid natural artworks against the backdrop of green.

Beyond Barry's Bay, we detour to Ōnawe Pā Historic Reserve, a nugget of land shaped like a tear drop, which on a map hangs like a pendant from the north shore of Akaroa Harbour. An island when the tide is high, the reserve was once occupied by a Māori fortress or *pā*. This morning, with the tide low, we cross from the mainland to the historic reserve on a narrow rocky ridge, its top pocked with tide pools. Once across, the ridge climbs steeply and exposes red clay flanks and nodding grasses and wildflowers. It broadens into a grassy hillock on which we can distinguish the *pā* only as long lines of dirt mounds with a single mound at the end of the reserve, nearest the ridge. Quickly, we scramble down the ridge to return to the mainland.

A dozen kilometres past the inland tip of Akaroa Harbour, we reach the small town of Akaroa, which nestles on the shore of French Bay and creeps back toward the slopes of ancient Akaroa Volcano. Although it's the largest urban centre on the harbour, the town bears no likeness whatsoever to Lyttelton. Whereas Lyttelton bustles with the action and noise inherent in a port town, Akaroa exudes a relaxed "summer home" atmosphere. French names adorning road signs are the legacy of settlers who arrived in 1840, only ten years after Te Rauparaha's murderous rampage during the Musket Wars, and mere days after the Union Jack was raised to proclaim British sovereignty. The French settlers chose to remain even under British rule, and their influence lives on.[111]

Beyond Akaroa, we follow the harbour's shore, then drive inland to a sheep station that's the trailhead for both Nīkau Palm Gully Track and the far longer Banks Peninsula Track, one of New Zealand's Great Walks. The hiking phase of our mission begins on the station's hilly pastures.

At its start, Nīkau Palm Gully Track is roomy and grazed by sheep less wary than most we've come across. It leads us over close-cropped grass and through thickets of *mānuka*, a low-growing tree that's considered to be a nursery species for regenerating forests although some farmers think it's a weed.[112] The boys climb, laughing, onto rounded sit-able shrubs. Some of the tiny-leaved plants thrust into the sky like bizarre sculptures.

SHEEP STATION, NĪKAU PALM GULLY TRACK

CLIMBING ON "SIT-ABLE" SHRUBS

In the pastures, we experience numerous close encounters of the woolly kind. Young sheep with undocked tails frolic like wild creatures on green slopes high above the magnetic blue of Akaroa Harbour. In the distance, gulls spin in circles around a fishing boat almost invisible on the harbour's turquoise. Beyond the boat, the massive, vertical cliffs of Timutimu Head, on the far side of the harbour, rise from the water.

As we approach the gully, the track skirts rocky cliffs and ends at a wooden gate. A stile beckons us over a fence, and we follow a narrow path down into a rare example of what remains of the native Banks Peninsula coastal forest. In single file, we slide down a slope of rich brown soil, descend a newly built ladder, and cling to vines and trees while slithering down a steep, rocky slope. Above us, leafy tree branches interlace to form a dense, shading canopy. The trunks of widely spaced *nīkau* palms, which Jānis has so much wanted to see, push up through the canopy like pale cement poles that end in upward-flaring clusters of leaves.

It's dark and dank beneath the forest's roof. Yellow and red containers labelled "DANGER POISON" hang from the trees, their poisoned baits intended for brushtail possums. Like many other feral mammals in this country, possums are fair game anytime and anywhere. They're colloquially called "coons," a fact Vilis discovered while reading Kiwi outdoorsman Charlie Janes's hunting and flying adventures in *Time for a Brew* and *Possum on a Cold Tin Roof.*[113] Photographs on the covers of Janes's books show a tanned man attired very much like the Ashley's Tow & Taxi driver, except that the driver's wool jersey is replaced by a camouflage jacket. Photographs within the books display airplanes, rifles, hunting dogs, and the carcasses of shot feral deer and pigs.

On the gully floor, we scramble over moss-covered boulders edging a rocky stream, lured by the sound of falling water. Around us, the coastal forest is a gloomy tangle of shrubs, ferns, and young *nīkau* with individual leaflets that are as long as Jānis is tall.

"Don't touch that tree!" I point to a tree nettle (*ongaonga*). Its many thin branches end in toothed leaves barbed with white stinging hairs. "See the hairs on the leaves? They can inject enough toxin to cause severe pain or, if someone touches a lot of them, even death. My guidebook says that horses and dogs have died after contact with tree nettle, and so did at least one tramper." That tramper decided the quickest route to a destination was through a stand of the toxic shrubs.[114]

JĀNIS AND YOUNG NĪKAU

Our upstream hike ends beside a pool at the base of a sheer wall. The cliff face is green with mosses and ferns and slick from moisture that falls a dozen metres and sounds like rain. The pool mesmerizes us, its blue-green colour emphasized by concentric ripples that emanate from its centre, into which the gentle waterfall spills. Shadows and moisture surround us. This sheltered forest is the antithesis of the exposed pastures through which we hiked to arrive here. In Nīkau Palm Gully, as in others like it between rocky headlands that drop to the ocean, we catch a glimpse of what existed before humans set foot on this land.

After our tramp, we return to Akaroa where we watch a glassblower shape exquisite vases from vivid coloured glass, and revel in the green fire of jade carvings displayed in art galleries. Red-billed gulls strut near a picnic table beside the harbour, hoping to share our *hoki* and chips beneath a sky so clear and sweet with warmth I wish the evening would never end.

My sons are cheerful and sweet, too, on the long drive to Lincoln. To relieve the tedium, we play the end-letter, beginning-letter word game, this time testing our alphabetical-Aotearoan acumen (Aotearoa is the Māori name for this country): *New Zealand. Democracy. Yellowhead. Dolphins. South Island. Dock. Kiwi. Irises. Sensational views. Song thrush. Hiwi the Kiwi. Impudent children. North Island. Dinner (not lunch). Raptors. Scotch broom. Mānuka. Akaroa...*

Hours later, in the darkness of Lincoln's oncoming night, we all stride to the rugby field to cap this day for Jānis. Leftover fireworks we bought for Guy Fawkes Day flame and sizzle against the night while my younger son dances with joy.

November 12

JUST AS days of rain characterized much of September in Canterbury, days of sun and clear skies have so far characterized much of November. Comfortably weary from our excursion to Nīkau Palm Gully yesterday, we choose an easy afternoon amble at The Groynes, a trio of ponds and wetlands formed by offshoots of Ōtukaikino

Creek, seven kilometres north of Christchurch.

Gravelled walkways guide us beneath towering willow trees, where resting ducks preen and sleep in shade near the water's edge. A loud, scratchy call attracts our attention to a family of Australian coots paddling with lobed feet among the reeds and grasses bordering a pond. The adults are sleek grey-and-black water birds with bright red eyes and white face shields and bills. Their two offspring sport fuzzy grey feathers, pinkish face shields, and tufts of sparse orange feathers atop their heads. Dainis photographs the coots and a raft of ducklings cruising the pond under the watchful eyes of a duck parent. Then the boys toss bits of grass and small daisies into the water, inciting mad dashes by the ducklings to be the first to grab up the tossed vegetation.

As we cross a bridge spanning Ōtukaikino Creek, we pass a cluster of Kiwi boys on the bridge who are egging each other to jump into the water. On the creek's far side, I identify a young lancewood tree by its thin, branchless trunk and narrow, serrated leaves that hang down. "It's called *horoeka* in Māori," I tell Vilis and the boys, my tree guide in hand. "Apparently, the leaves' midribs were sometimes used by settlers as boot laces or to mend harness."[115]

"Really?" Vilis clips off a lancewood leaf with his pocket knife, cuts out its midrib, unlaces his sneaker, and re-laces it with the lancewood lace. "It works."

I also spot a small pepper tree with its characteristic yellow-green leaves highlighted by red-edged, see-through holes. I crush a leaf that releases a strong, peppery aroma. "Smell this," I tell the boys.

"Whoa! Strong or what?" Dainis exclaims.

"The leaves are supposed to taste like pepper and were used to relieve pain by the Māori. They call it *horopito*."[116] We continue along the creek past clumps of flax, cabbage trees, and *whēkī*, a kind of stout tree fern with a thick trunk and huge skirt of dead leaves.

Our outing ends too quickly, so we link up with Waimairi Walkway, a loop track that leads us along the edges of farm fields and through pastures. After our exciting scramble down and up Nīkau Palm Gully yesterday and our long tramp through pastures overlooking majestic Akaroa Harbour, the Waimairi loop seems tame and nondescript – even unsettling as we skirt a sprayed paddock having vegetation as dead and grey as the plants we observed on the hillside near Woolshed Creek last month. Sadness invades me – sadness that a country blessed with so many natural riches seems to so freely lace its environment with poisons. Suddenly I want to be somewhere else, somewhere far from Canterbury's agricultural landscape with its conspicuous dead strips of plants adjacent to ditches, walls, fences, and hedges.

Vilis, however, photographs stiles to add to his Stiles of New Zealand Collection: a stile crossing a weathered board fence, a stile crossing an electric fence, a stile leading to thin air, and lastly, a rubber-coated stile leading to Poplar Avenue.

Here, the track narrows into a dirt path dwarfed by a double row of gigantic Lombardi poplars. From a distance, the tall poplars had appeared as nothing more than an effective windbreak. Now, as we stand before them, they take our breaths away. Like massive, age-worn pillars bearing a cathedral roof of leaves and sky, or like two regiments of colossal soldiers standing at attention while facing each other, their grey fissured trunks guard the narrow track that passes serenely between them. Hushed, we gaze up in awe as we walk the path between the pillars, between the soldiers. Then, unwilling to leave the majestic poplars so soon, we retrace our steps to the stile and walk the path again.

POPLAR AVENUE

November 14

A ROILING mass of grey cloud to the south of Lincoln moves in fast, the cloud's lower stratum rolling over on itself like dirty surf pounding onto a storm-battered beach. Thunder rumbles, and lightning splits the sky. Vilis looks up from where he's replacing missing screws in the Bomb's right rear door liner. He nods to the sky. "You can tell there's something ugly in that."

A chill runs through me at the thought of twenty exuberant Cubs doing sprints, ball throws, long jumps, and high jumps during a lightning storm. "I'm going back up to the school," I tell Vilis, then hurry along North Belt.

Rain spatters the sidewalk, and gusting wind shoves me. By the time I reach Lincoln Primary, the sky is wild with swirling, billowing thunderheads and electric flashes. The Cubs are still out on the field. When I look for Jānis, I spot him near the high jump. "I think they should come in," I call to one of the Cub leaders, who's placing equipment in the shelter of the school's veranda. "They're out in the middle of a soccer field and there's fork lightning all around."

"We probably should call it," he agrees.

The wind pushes harder at my back as we run across the field to the high jump. We have to holler that everyone should take shelter. Andrew looks up at the sky and agrees. The leaders yell and motion to the Cubs to run to the school's veranda. As Jānis and I run together, a giant slap of wind hits us within a dozen steps of the high jump. It pelts us with rain and bits of ice. "There's *hail!*" Jānis yells up to me.

Excited Cubs scream and stream across the field in a dark green tide. In the shelter of the school's veranda, we stand shivering while the clouds empty their icy guts onto the field. Cubs dash out into the storm to collect hail and squash it into balls to throw at one another. "Look, there's a rainbow!" a Cub calls, and the message passes the length of the veranda. Within a dozen minutes of the first hailstone, the storm abates.

Back at Lincoln Domain, Cubs scoop up handfuls of hail blown against a corrugated metal wall and pelt each other with icy missiles. They're still wild, as though the storm infected them with some of its explosive energy. Inside the hall, Scouts check their equipment in preparation for a backpacking excursion to Mount Somers on the upcoming weekend. Dainis is in the thick of things, alight with drive and focused energy. Action sizzles all around me, the Scout Hall and its grounds…a cauldron of stewing, youthful enthusiasm.

November 16

CUT GRASS lies in neat swaths on farmers' fields, green-gold in the morning sun. When I drive to Christchurch for skating, I also see familiar rows of large, circular grass bales neatly wrapped with sturdy white plastic, and a hill of packed grass covered with plastic and weighted with old tires – the grass in both on its way to becoming silage. Completely absent from the rural landscape, however, are the tall, round-topped silos still commonly used in Canada to produce silage. I envision them rising high above dairy farms perched atop the hills of Nova Scotia's Shubenacadie River Valley, like castles rising up through the mists of the Rhine. Haying, or in this case, making silage, truly heralds the onset of summer. It's peculiar, though, to have that summer begin in November, a month when my family is much more accustomed to getting our cross-country skis from storage and equipping our vehicles with studded tires for winter driving.

THIS EVENING, an interesting statistic comes to light when Vilis reads the *Christchurch Mail* after tea. "Listen to this. Three-quarters of the population of New Zealand lives on the North Island." He looks up at me and adds that one of his co-workers said she never enjoys her trips to North Island because there are people everywhere. She told him she much prefers South Island. "So maybe we won't be sad that we have only six weeks there," he adds.

New Zealand's population is about 3.6 million,[117] so about 2.7 million Kiwis call North Island home. Most live in Auckland and Wellington,[118] and those cities hold only passing interest for Vilis and me. As friendly and generous as many of the Kiwis we've met have been, it's this country's land and its plants and animals that he and I have come here to experience.

However, as the days and weeks pass, it's become clear that the same is not true for our sons. As much as Dainis and Jānis appreciate the physical challenges of our outdoor adventures, they still need time to make and explore connections with other children. How will they respond to our time on North Island, where they'll live and work with adults? They'll have no Cubs or Scouts and no skating or tennis. Will the lure of the rainforest be enough?

November 17

THIS MORNING, Dainis's backpack bulges with extra clothes and his assigned portion of the Lincoln Scout Troop's camping supplies. He grins and strides away from North Belt into the adventure of a weekend of tramping and camping on Mount Somers.

Vilis, Jānis, and I spend the morning and afternoon at The Canterbury Show, a regional agricultural exhibition that features a mind-boggling array of events, domestic animals, and wool samples with fibres described in terms of microns. Farriers face-off in a shoeing competition. Burly men lift stone balls weighing a hundred kilograms and more. Huge barns are filled with sheep: Lincoln, Leicester, Romney, Merino, Suffolk, Hampshire, and other breeds. The Supreme Grand Champion Merino ram is huge and magnificent, with wool so deep and thick, his eyes are barely visible.

A stadium near the barns hosts a sheep-shearing competition in which six men compete in heats. Each shearer shears four sheep. As far as I can determine, the correct shearing sequence is foreleg and rear leg on one side of the sheep in order to free the fleece, then the head and neck, followed by the side and back, and then the sheep's opposite side. Vilis times several shearers, each of whom requires about a minute and a half to grab and shear a sheep. The action is imbued with the same riveting intensity as calf roping or steer wrestling in a North American rodeo. I love it!

In a venue overflowing with food vendors, I order a barbecued whitebait sandwich, keen to try it. The boys and I have learned of the little fishes in our new reading book, Margaret Hall's historical novel *Swag and Tucker*, which is set on the West Coast during New Zealand's gold rush years.[119] When the sandwich arrives, Vilis cuts it into three pieces, and he, Jānis, and I bite into slabs of white bread that hold tiny, batter-coated, grilled whitebait. The taste is mild against the plain bread, and we rate the piscine sandwich as mediocre for our tastes. Vilis and Jānis also sample ostrich burgers, which they enjoy, the dark meat tasting "a little like duck," according to Vilis. I choose a venison and bacon burger, and find the spicy sauce on the burger rather overpowering.

During the afternoon, we lose our hearts to gentle, soft-haired alpacas, and I return to the vendors' display to buy jars of honeydew and *mānuka* honey. Outdoors again, our attention is caught by elegant riders on hunters competing in Canterbury Arena. We join a crowd seated on a grassy slope and enjoy watching the horses and riders in action. Children roll down the slope while my hands turn purple in the cold air. Beside me, Vilis is in shorts and coughing.

At the completion of the equestrian event, a helicopter drones in over the arena and hovers hundreds of metres above the ground. Spooked hunters snort and prance away from the arena. An announcer blares that David, a member of The Canterbury Show's organizing committee, will bungy jump from the helicopter.

As the crowd gapes upward, a man climbs through an open door in the helicopter and onto the chopper's ski. Wind whips his hair as he clings to the fuselage. I can't imagine leaping into thin air from such a height without a parachute, but after a few seconds surveying the scene below him, David flings himself off the chopper. His body plunges down toward the ground, and coils of pale, thick rope follow him. The rope is attached to the chopper at one end, and to David's legs at the other. It straightens as he falls. When the rope reaches its maximum length, David bounces up and down like a yo-yo, metres above the grass. The rope is obviously elastic. Along with the rest of the crowd, we burst into cheers and applause as the helicopter pilot lowers David gently to the ground.

After the rope is off the jumper's legs, the chopper pulsates away and the announcer rushes over to David and asks him, "So, what did you think when you were up there at a thousand feet?"

"Bloody high," breathless David answers.

Vilis coughs more and more while we watch a military peacekeepers' demonstration in the arena, during which a patrol, moving into "new territory" to rescue refugees, carries out highly structured manoeuvres. After the soldiers retrieve the refugees, they disguise their retreat with a screen of coloured smoke, delighting Jānis. In the distance beyond the plumes of red and blue smoke, the

Port Hills are shrouded in menacing purple-grey clouds as likely to hold snow as rain. Miserably cold, we call it quits in mid-afternoon and wonder how the Scouts are faring.

At 5:57 p.m., Vilis realizes that the Royal New Zealand Ballet's performance of *Cinderella*, for which we bought tickets, is scheduled to begin at 6:30 p.m. and not 7:30 p.m. as he had assumed. We abandon dishes on the table and sprint to the car. Jānis is still dressed in the shorts and T-shirt he wore to The Canterbury Show, Vilis sports a purple Save the Rainforest T-shirt, and I'm wearing a blouse and jeans.

In Christchurch, traffic lights change agonizingly slowly. Finally, Vilis slides the car in beside Theatre Royal, and Jānis and I scramble out to collect our tickets while Vilis finds parking. Tickets in hand, we wait for Vilis, but too soon a disembodied voice within the theatre announces it's time to take our seats. The foyer empties rapidly, with many guests hurrying to climb the stairs and enter the theatre's dress circle and gallery. I spot an official-looking man in a suit standing on the stairs, looking out over the foyer. I rush to him and explain, "My husband isn't here yet. He's parking the car, and it's time for us to go in. What should I do?"

With businesslike composure, he responds, "Leave a ticket with me. I'll see he gets it. What's his name?"

"Vilis Nams." I show him the name printed on the ticket reserve slip and hand him the ticket. Then Jānis and I mount the stairs and enter the gallery Row C of Theatre Royal (now Isaac Theatre Royal).

Ninety-two years old and steeped in Edwardian style,[120] this theatre is the opposite of the futuristic Christchurch Town Hall Auditorium in which my family heard the Christchurch Symphony Orchestra perform three weeks ago. That venue reverberated with sharp contrast and colour. This one is cozy and comfortable in subdued lighting, its age reflected in the walls' ornate decorative trim. Our seats high above the stage grant us a clear view of the theatre's domed ceiling, alive with lushly painted scenes reminiscent of those I've seen on the ceilings of European castles and cathedrals. The instant before the theatre doors close, Vilis slips into his seat beside me. Panting, he tells me, "I ran three blocks from a car park."

As the ballet proceeds, Jānis and I are struck by the visual similarities between this dance form and figure skating: the powerful jumps with multiple rotations, the strength, the elegance. Thirty minutes into the performance, small red lights flash on the theatre walls. Members of the audience rise from their seats and move toward exits. The performers leave the stage, and it dawns on Vilis and me that the red lights are a silent fire alarm. We join the rest of the audience exiting the building.

Outside, we wait in spitting rain near a cluster of musicians from the New Zealand Symphony Orchestra who provided live accompaniment for the ballet. Dressed in black, they shield their instruments protectively. When the all-clear signal is given, we re-enter the dim theatre, wherein lissom, red-haired Cinderella resumes her resting position of despair on her wicked stepmother's hearth.

November 18

FOR THE first time since we arrived in New Zealand, the Port Hills are dusted with snow. We can only assume Mount Somers is as well. Again, I wonder how the Scouts are faring.

In mid-morning, Vilis, Jānis, and I explore Coes Ford on Selwyn River southwest of Lincoln, searching for fish and birds. The shallow river runs over a gravel bed, and we catch glimpses of brown trout travelling its liquid highway. With the exception of a lone cabbage tree, the vegetation lining the river's banks (willows, grasses, young poplars) could be found almost anywhere in North America. Flood debris, caught high in trees, indicates a three-metre rise in water levels during past flooding. It occurs to me that perhaps it was Selwyn River that flooded highways south of Christchurch in late August.

Fluffy willow seeds drift onto the water. Male chaffinches, perched in willow trees, sing stuttering songs, like a long line of hesitant minstrels. A grey duck and her seven ducklings swim by near the far shore, keeping to the cover offered by drooping willow branches that create green reflections on the water. Open fields behind us resonate with birdsong and sheep bleats.

We wade across a tributary (ice cold on our feet) and explore an adjacent field bright with orange and yellow poppies. Scotch broom bears fading flowers and fuzzy seed pods, and we can hear gorse seed pods pop in the warm sunshine. Debris hangs from a fence thirty metres from the river, more evidence of flooding.

We return to the Selwyn and push through rank vegetation. I pause amid thick grasses to look for birds while Vilis and Jānis continue upstream hoping to catch some trout. An Australasian harrier swoops overhead, causing the grey duck hen to quickly shoo her family behind a screen of overhanging leaves. The harrier is one of only a few native bird species to benefit from the arrival of humans in New Zealand, since people brought mammals and new birds the hawk could add to its menu.

Like the ducks, I also seek cover beneath a willow umbrella, but to avoid rain rather than raptor. Hail arrives with Vilis and Jānis, even while patches of blue light the sky. After the hail abates, we hike to the car and head for Lincoln, knowing that our friends, Betty and Colin, will return from their national park explorations today.

During the evening, Colin regales us with details of his and Betty's travels. He describes Abel Tasman National Park's golden sands, North Island's protected *kauri* forests, and the Tongariro Alpine Crossing's barren volcanic craters. His words set flames to the dry wood of my tramping desires.

November 19

THE SOUR smell of fermenting honeydew permeates beech stands in Oxford Forest, about sixty kilometres northwest of Lincoln. White-flowering clumps of *puawānanga* (clematis) hang from the trees in showy bouquets. Once worn as elegant headdresses by Māori women, clematis flowers are the crowing glory of vines that creep their way upward in the forest through the use of touch-sensitive leaf stalks.[121]

On our hike du jour, the track leads Vilis, Colin, Betty, Jānis, and me along a ridge that offers views of vast, steep hillsides thick with native beech forest so green and dark it creates a yearning to stay and make our way into that dark, tempting woodland. Too soon, however, we must retrace our steps and return to Lincoln, for a certain Canadian youth is on his way home from the Mount Somers Scout outing.

Dainis's laughter, unheard for three days, is a bright, beloved sound in the house. He tells us of his adventures: of rain that poured onto the Scouts while they tramped uphill and downhill and crossed a river before slogging up to Pinnacles Hut on Mount Somers. Later, he wrote this in his Scouting diary:

Then we had sausages-in-bread for lunch, and I hung my clothes to dry, since it poured the whole hike in.

"The hut was really crowded by evening," he says. "There were twenty-six people! One was only five years old." (They start them young in this country!)

Then it started snowing, and snowing, and snowing! In the morning, there were eight inches of snow on the ground! Our leaders decided not to go on to Woolshed Hut, but to stay at Pinnacles because of the snow. We had a great snowball fight the whole morning!

He laughs. "One of the Scouts wanted his Nintendo and Game Boy! By evening, seven trampers had left the hut, so it wasn't so crowded anymore."

Of today, he wrote this:

We had porridge for breakfast this morning, then packed up all our gear. We had a brunch of pikelets, and then hiked out. I fell into the river while crossing, but we had a barbecue at the end, which was good.

"So, Dainis, what did you think of it, overall?" Vilis asks.

Our son nods firmly. "It was hard, but fun."

November 20

SELWYN RIVER again flows serenely beneath Coes Ford as the boys and I join two homeschooling families for a picnic on the river's pebbly shore. My sons and the four other children, all of whom are younger than Dainis and Jānis, are drawn to the river's smoothly flowing water. As if guided by some instinct, they gather flat, smooth skipping stones and fling them side-arm across the water. Their lilting voices discuss shapes, grips, throwing angles, and they count the number of skips. I join them, and my first attempts are dismal failures. Then I find a perfect skipping stone (flat, round, thin) and exclaim with as much delight as the children when it dances across the water.

Two more families join us, and the talk among the adults (all women) skips from where exactly Nova Scotia is and what the weather would be like there at this time of year (wet, wet, wet, according to recent e-mails) to the regulations for homeschooling in Canada and New Zealand. Over lunch, I'm asked countless questions. Why did I start homeschooling? Are there support groups for homeschoolers in Canada? Is Nova Scotia bilingual? Would I ever need to use French in day-to-day life? I, in turn, ask whether children here are required to learn a second language. "I think they have the option when they're in high school," one of the women replies.

Another responds, "If there was a required language, it would probably be Māori."

"Yes," the first agrees, "but it's a dead language."

"It is?" I ask. "No one speaks it?"

"Oh, you hear five minutes of it on the radio every day, but that's it. I've never heard anyone actually use it."

"Interesting," I comment. "At Landcare, the receptionist always answers the phone by saying, '*Kia ora.* Landcare Research.'"

The river runs quietly. Jānis wades in its centre, his bare legs white, his cargo pants hitched high on his thighs. Dainis curls into a ball on the sweatshirt he laid on the pebbles beside me, weary from his weekend Scouting expedition. I gather our empty sandwich boxes and call Jānis in from the river. We say our farewells, knowing there'll be more homeschool gatherings. I feel at peace knowing my family is not alone in this educational choice, even in a foreign country.

On our return to Lincoln, the house oozes silence. Betty and Colin boarded their flight to Canada this morning and soon after, Vilis caught an interisland flight to Wellington. By now, he's at Ōwhango, probably driving a quad on pitted tracks through the Tongariro Forest Conservation Area. He'll spend the next four days at the stoat research site before returning to Lincoln. That will give us a day to prepare for a week-long excursion to Queenstown, in the neighbouring province of Otago. While Vilis attends a Pacific

Wildlife Conference, the boys and I will hike Queenstown tracks and explore the self-proclaimed "Adventure Capital of the World."

November 21

DAWN ARRIVES early now, the sky already brightening at 4:50 a.m. The Port Hills' slanted peaks are black cusps against streaks of hot pink and deep blue when I drive to the rink for Jānis's early skate. Today, I'm the chauffeur, since Vilis is on North Island for three more days.

The rink is peaceful, its air cool and still. Silence is broken by sporadic chatter, the slick scrape of blades on ice, and the dull thuds of bladed boots landing after jumps. While Jānis practices axel landings in the jumping harness, I watch from high in the stands and write notes to family in Canada, on postcards that portray New Zealand scenes of vivid blue water and lush green plants. Dainis watches *Tin Tin* on television in Zamboni's.

Then I skate while the boys work diligently at their homeschool assignments and sip marshmallow-topped hot chocolate in the warm room. I keep them close while Vilis is away, but right now, I revel in the ice surface between us. I'm a person who needs physical space and time to myself.

Back at home, I make a list of supplies we'll need for our Queenstown trip and outline a travel plan for our excursion, the longest since our arrival in New Zealand and the last multi-day tour before we leave for North Island. To date, we've scored two of Jānis's three *P*s (parrots and palm trees) and on this trip into new territory in South Island's southern half, we hope to score the third *P*, penguins, which we all want to see.

We'll travel south along the East Coast to Oamaru and its penguin colonies, then swing west to drive through interior Otago to

Queenstown, which nestles on Lake Wakatipu. Our return drive will take us north through the centre of South Island, another new route for us. Since the weather has warmed up and dried out significantly during the past few weeks, we'll tent in campgrounds during our travels, and stay at the Queenstown hotel hosting the wildlife conference. I've researched tracks for the boys and me to hike in the Queenstown area and am keen to trail ride in the shadow of the Southern Alps. New landscapes. New experiences. All will help us piece together more of the geographical, ecological, and cultural puzzle that's New Zealand.

November 25

YESTERDAY, CATHEDRAL Square in downtown Christchurch was mottled with the tents and tables of craft vendors, and souvenir stores were busy with customers. The boys and Vilis accompanied me while I purchased lightweight Christmas gifts to mail to Canada: sheep's wool slippers for my mother, possum wool gloves for my brothers, and brooches, pendants, and earrings crafted from swirling, iridescent blue and green *pāua* (abalone) shell for my sisters.

This morning, the rush of wrapping gifts and writing Christmas cards is exhausting, but at 11:00 a.m., the post office attendant in Lincoln takes two large boxes off my hands with assurances they'll arrive before December 25th. When I return to the bungalow, I'm greeted by the clutter of supplies for our Queenstown trip: packs, tent, cooler, boxes of food.

While we eat lunch, Vilis tinkers with the toaster, attempting to make an adjustment with his pocket knife. "Ow!" he yelps. Blood runs down his left hand and spatters onto the floor. He clasps his right hand over the cut and asks me in a strained voice, "Can you get me a bandage? It's about two inches long."

I slap a pressure bandage over a gaping wound that's much wider than I expected. It's not a neat slice. Rather, it's a gash that's deep and bloody at one end and shallow and wide at the other, as though the knife blade jabbed in and then sliced sideways under the skin.

My husband sits down, his face green.

I quickly arrange to bring him to the Lincoln Medical Centre, where twenty-four-hour, on-call medical service is available. As I guide him toward the door, I leave the boys with instructions to wash the dishes and wait *carefully*. No wild romping. We don't need any more accidents on the verge of our trip.

At the clinic, I fill out forms while the tall, blond on-call doctor removes the blood-stained bandage from Vilis's hand. "It's bleeding like billy-o!" she exclaims cheerfully before cleaning and examining the wound. Then she injects the tissues around it with local anaesthetic and with adrenaline to cause blood vessels to spasm and control bleeding. "I can't anaesthetize until after examining, because it distorts the tissues," she explains apologetically to Vilis. She shows me the deep end of the wound and the tendon to Vilis's index finger, which the knife blade barely missed. In the shallow, wide end of the wound, I see glistening silvery bubbles of subcutaneous fat. Abruptly, I sit back on my chair, my composure starting to slip.

"Do you want to look at it?" the doctor asks Vilis.

"No."

"I probably wouldn't either. I can look inside anybody else's hands, but I don't think I'd want to look inside mine." While the anaesthetic takes hold, she gives Vilis a tetanus shot. Then she sews the edges of the gaping wound together with seven neat stitches, telling my husband, "At first, I thought I might have to send you to the plastic people." As she tidies up, she smiles at him. "If you want to think of yourself as lucky, then you could say that you're lucky today."

We thank the doctor, then depart for Queenstown, two hours later than planned. I drive with Vilis beside me, his left arm in a sling and his pain knocked into submission by Extra Strength Tylenol. South of Lincoln, scattered shrub lupins (another invasive introduced plant) edge the highway, their yellow flowers shouting that summer has arrived in Canterbury. The road carries us over the stony bellies of the Rakaia, Ashburton, and Rangitata Rivers. Beyond Geraldine, it leads us east to the coast, where we head south to our destination for today, Oamaru and its colonies of yellow-eyed penguins and blue penguins. In the coastal town, the boys and I erect our tent in a crowded campground adjacent to Oamaru Gardens. Then I drive us to Bushy Beach, a birding hotspot for yellow-eyed penguins.

BUSHY BEACH

The beach is a long sand crescent backed by steep slopes covered with scrub, grasses, herbs, and flax clumps. From a track leading upward along a hillside, we spot a penguin emerging from the ocean. The torpedo-shaped bird waddles from side to side. Its legs and feet are thick and pink, and its flippers are thinner than I expected.

A wild scream draws our attention away from that penguin and rivets it onto a yellow-eyed penguin standing at the base of a flax clump only ten metres from the trail. With wings held outward and beak raised, the bird emits a shrieking whistle. Its yellow eyes and the broad yellow stripe across its head are clearly visible, as is a silver band attached to its right flipper. This species (*Megadyptes antipodes*) is the world's rarest penguin, so seeing it up close is a thrill.

From an interpretive display in a blind farther along the track, we learn that yellow-eyed penguins breed as far north as Banks Peninsula, and that they can swim forty kilometres out to sea and dive two hundred metres deep to catch their prey. From the blind, we scan the shore and spot a vertical black and white shape on the edge of a rock outcrop far down the beach. We also notice another penguin climbing partway up a hillside, plus the one that earlier emerged from the surf. Apparently the last is in no hurry to reach its nesting burrow. It pauses often to preen its glistening black-and-white jacket.

Hours later, at 9:30 p.m., we see a raft of the world's smallest penguins, blue penguins, appear as a dark blur about two hundred metres away in Oamaru Harbour. Gradually, the raft approaches shore, where my family and a crowd of other penguin-watchers have gathered at a commercial viewing site.

The blue penguins ride the water and swim like seals beneath its surface. In kelp beds near shore, they look like dark, moving shadows. Surf tosses them onto the beach, where they scramble to their feet and waddle toward a road's rocky base. Two penguins swim far to the left of the others and are washed in among rocks. Once, twice, thrice they swim back out into the surf and attempt another landing, only to repeat their rocky come-ashore. Finally, they swim out far enough to distance themselves from the rocks and catch a wave onto the sand.

Unlike the yellow-eyed penguins, which maintained a relatively upright posture when walking, the blues lean forward as they propel their plump bodies across the sand. When they pause to preen, their wet feathers shine like fish scales in the orange glow of street lights illuminating the harbour road.

After preening, the blue penguins cross the road and slip through a page wire fence that protects their nest sites. Some penguins arrow to nest boxes set into mounds of earth, while others climb a dirt cliff to their burrows. From various sites on the cliff, growls and croaks erupt into the darkness, the penguins' voices loud against the calm night air.

It amazes me that, even with the lights, road, and crowd of people here in Oamaru, these ancient birds still follow their homing instinct to their nesting ground. Meanwhile, out on the swelling waves of the Pacific, still more rafts of little blues (the remainder of the colony) are dark shadows swimming to shore.

November 26

A PEACOCK'S scream splits the morning air in Oamaru Gardens. The sound is in nerve-jangling contrast to songbirds' more serene voices. My family strolls through the gardens and checks out the aviaries, which hold pigeons and parakeets. Two peacocks display to each other, their raised tail feathers liquid blue-and-green silver. Near the duck pond, an interpretive sign quotes a passage from New Zealand writer, Janet Frame's novel, *Owls Do Cry*, published in 1957.[122] As a writer, I drink in the evocative words:

> Now this Saturday was the first of May, the opening of the shooting season, and the evening papers would be full of photographs of men in gumboots and waterproof jackets leaning on rifles, and holding high the twisted neck and wet body of swan or goose or wild paradise duck that gleams blue and green like a split rainbow. And it had seemed that all night before, and early in the morning, the ducks had been flying over, low in the mist below the clouds, to find shelter in the town gardens where they mingled with their tamed and plump relatives, and with them, on the special duck pond at the garden, were chased and stoned by children and choked with the million white-bread crumbs of their charity...

Nominated for the Nobel Prize in Literature, Frame is considered New Zealand's most celebrated writer. She lived part of her life in Oamaru and incorporated disguised locales within the town (Oamaru Gardens, for example) into her fiction.[123]

From Oamaru, we travel south to where the Moeraki Boulders lie like giant stone eyeballs scattered across Moeraki Beach. Some of the boulders are small – the eyeballs of infant giants – and some bulge a metre and a half above the sand. The latter dwarf Dainis and Jānis when the boys duck behind the rock spheres.

Moments later, my sons peek out with grins on their faces.

Nearby shattered boulders reveal internal honeycombed structures of amber-coloured crystals. The boys scramble atop intact boulders and collect pebbles eroded from the broken honeycombs. Vilis strolls with me along the shore, his left arm elevated in a sling. The bandage covering his hand is dark with dried blood. His wound still hurts, but elevating eases the pain.

AT MORAKI BEACH

Leaving Moeraki Beach behind, we travel farther south along the coast to the small town of Palmerston and then inland away from the ocean. The highway twists and climbs over rolling, grassy hills. Dry mountains thrust up in the background. Some have the striking conical shape we've seen in the Port Hills. In Ranfurly, we pause for lime ice cream cones to soothe our throats in the afternoon heat. The station wagon doesn't have air conditioning, so it's a relief to take a break from its "oven."

While licking my cone, I notice a poster on the side of a hotel. It's emblazoned with the words "SOUTHERN MAN" and depicts a tanned man with hands on hips standing beside his horse in a setting that could be anywhere on this grassy interior plateau.

The poster reminds me of the old Marlborough Man cigarette ads in North American magazines, except that the southern man doesn't wear jeans and a western shirt, nor cowboy boots and a cowboy hat. Instead, he wears shorts, a singlet (sleeveless undershirt), wool socks, and short, lace-up boots. A shirt (must be a swandri, one of those plaid hunting shirts) is tied around his waist, and three dogs rest at his feet. He looks fit, strong, and self-reliant, his physical appearance embodying the rugged qualities of the land displayed behind him. Unlike the Marlborough Man, he's not promoting smoking. Instead, he's an advertisement for Speight's beer. Early twentieth-century New Zealand literature portrayed Kiwi men as tough loners, outdoorsmen or farmers who treated women and cities with equal awkwardness.[124] Perhaps the southern man represents the modern version.

Between Ranfurly and Alexandra, I steer the Bomb through eighty-six kilometres of twists and climbs and battle her recalcitrant gears and sluggish engine. The heat is stifling. Near Alexandra the plateau country gives way to orchards and dry badlands bordering Manuherikia River Valley. This central part of Otago is as landlocked as any terrain gets in New Zealand. Its climate has all the features of a continental climate that lacks ameliorating ocean influences. It's hotter, colder, and drier than anywhere else in the country. This combination of climatic factors encourages the growth of grasslands, which we've seen in abundance, and of top-quality wine grapes in what are the most southerly vineyards in the world.[125]

We're too late to catch the information centre in Alexandra while it's open, however, a map on its window indicates the location of two campgrounds. Three notices taped to the centre's glass doors seek workers to thin nectarine, cherry, and apple crops. Another notice advertises A. J. Hackett Bungy near Queenstown. Off in the distance, we hear the gunshot-like booms of bird scarers in orchards.

We choose a campground beside the river, where huge willows drape graceful, thickly leaved branches over our grassy tent site. After tea, we step down the bank behind our tent and pass through the willow curtain to walk beside the river. Pied stilts and spur-winged plovers bob and peck among pebbles on a gravel bar. Dainis and Jānis fling stones into the water. After returning through the willows, we creep around the face of a rock wall that juts into the river, climb the outcrop, and toss pebbles into the water running deep and black below.

November 27

JĀNIS SPUTTERS, "That was cold!" He shivers while dashing from the river to the tent to change into dry clothes. He alone braved the river for a wake-up dip. (Vilis would have, but couldn't because of his stitches.) This son is a thrill seeker. He'd make a good Kiwi.

After breaking camp, we leave the car in shade near Alexandra's information centre and obtain a tramping map from the centre's attendant. The young woman indicates the route to Shaky Bridge, the start of the Alexandra–Clyde Track. She tells us, "You can walk anywhere you want on the hills across the river. They're covered with old gold mine tailings."

OTAGO'S GOLD RUSH

The lure of gold brought thousands of prospectors to New Zealand during the second half of the nineteenth century. Central Otago's gold rush was the country's largest and attracted prospectors from Australia, China, Europe, and North America. Between 1861 and 1864, Otago's population tripled. The wealth dug from the province's hills and mountains made the coastal city of Dunedin the country's largest for a time and also financed New Zealand's first university, the University of Otago. [126]

We cross Manuherikia River and follow a dirt road past a vineyard. The scent of thyme surprises me, and I notice mauve-tinted clumps of the herb growing amid grasses and the first wild roses we've seen in this country. We turn off the dirt road onto a path and climb toward Clock on the Hill, a massive metal clock face high above the river and town.

ON A THYME-COVERED HILL ABOVE ALEXANDRA

An easy walk at the start, the excursion morphs into a scramble over broken rock near the hill's summit. From a distance, I'd thought the slopes were barren scree. Instead, they're covered with thyme, which has colonized the rough piles of mine tailings on this side of the river as far as the eye can see. Thyme is yet another introduced plant gone wildly astray in New Zealand. Our stomachs roil from its overpowering fragrance.

Clock on the Hill dwarfs us, its eleven-metre diameter undoubtedly making it visible for several kilometres. The clock face and hour markers are equipped with small electric bulbs that light up at night. Far below us, Alexandra's pale buildings and dark trees cling to a gravely smile of the river. After descending the hill, we cross the river, sucking in air to clean the reek of thyme from our lungs.

Later, while we stroll Alexandra's streets, I notice Christmas wishes painted on store windows in neon hues of purple, green, and hot pink. I envision the classic red, white, and dark green of popular North American Christmas colours. "Do you suppose it's because it's hot here?" I ask Vilis.

With less than a month remaining before Christmas, we've seen little evidence of holiday preparations. Here, the celebration falls in the heat of summer's longest days when crops and gardens are ripening and livestock fattening, thus demanding time and attention from farmers and gardeners. Perhaps the overall lushness of the season is what fans some Kiwis' appetites for showy colours.

"Did I ever tell you the story of what Andrea and Andy did the first winter they spent in Vancouver?" Vilis asks.

"No."

"They missed the heat so much that they drove all the way down to California so they could spend Christmas Day on a hot beach!"

I laugh and think of a Christmas Day at home in Nova Scotia: short daylight, cold temperatures, and often, snow. To us, a long, hot Christmas Day seems bizarre.

From Alexandra, we travel north past Clyde and its dam on the Kawarau River, built to create the vast reservoir of Lake Dunstan, then head west beside the river. I pull off at Roaring Meg Power Station, where we gaze down at churning rapids in Kawarau Gorge.

KAWARAU GORGE

A van hauling a trailer also turns into the parking area. Figures in black wet suits emerge from the van, and the driver unlocks the trailer. The river surfers don helmets and buoyancy vests. Then, carrying rubber flippers and dense foam sledges, they scramble down a rocky slope to an eddy in the river. There, they tug on flippers and receive a training session in river surfing.

I strike up a conversation with the driver, who stands watching the surfers. "Where are they from?" I ask.

Amiable and a bit dishevelled, he replies, "Three Germans, two Welsh, one Swede, three New Zealanders, and there's one whose accent I can't place. Two of them are women."

"How long will they ride the river?"

"About an hour. They'll go through three big rapids: Maneater, Rollercoaster – that's about five hundred metres of standing waves – and Dead Cow." He mentions that the river surfing business is based in Queenstown. "It's a very dear [expensive] place to live. I'm actually living in a tent in a campground right now."

So, this is our first glimpse into the thrill seeker's paradise of Queenstown.

Our second glimpse comes in the form of the Kawarau Suspension Bridge and A. J. Hackett Bungy, the original forty-three-metre bungy jump northeast of Queenstown, and the first commercial bungy jump in the world. From a viewing platform, we and busloads of other spectators watch as jumpers – men and women – inch forward on the bridge to a projecting plank. It's a scene reminiscent of every walk-the-plank episode ever read about or seen on the silver screen.

When each jumper reaches the plank, a thick white elastic cable attached to the bridge is fastened around his or her lower legs by a narrow, strap-like cord. Some of the jumpers readily shuffle forward to the plank's edge and dive into the air above the river. Others, their faces white with terror, stand like zombies and are pushed off the plank. They scream on their descent. All are, in turn, retrieved by the pilot of a tethered inflatable raft floating on the river. Vilis is tempted to try the jump, but in the end decides he'd rather not take the chance of detaching his retina. (Apparently, eye injuries may occur due to increased blood pressure in the head when the elastic cable rebounds.)

On the last leg to Queenstown, the pavement beneath the car's tires reeks of oily asphalt in the boiling heat. Near the adventure town, we're refreshed by views of soaring, saw-toothed mountains and blue Lake Wakatipu. Queenstown itself crowds the shore of the lake and lies at the base of forested hills.

After some confusion, we locate Rydges, the hotel hosting the Pacific Wildlife Conference. It's face is impressive, with white pillars rising into arches below a black flat-topped roof hinting at a Mediterranean influence. From our room's balcony, we gaze out at a spectacular view of mountains and lake. Two jet boats speed over the water, and a paraglider floats in the sky, blue parachute billowing gently. Against the majestic backdrop shaped by sideswiping tectonic plates and gouging glaciers, the thrill seekers look small and busy, like gnats.

November 28

DRIZZLE DRIPS onto the boys and me. We wander downtown to explore Queenstown shops, which are primarily upscale and geared to tourists. We enter a jewellery store advertising black pearls (a novelty to us) and study the dark green spheres shimmering on satin beds. An elegantly clad woman with a French accent enthusiastically answers all our questions. She tells us that the pearls were produced by green-lipped oysters farmed in Tahitian lagoons and describes how the oysters' free-swimming larvae settle onto mesh hung within the lagoons. After three years, the oysters are seeded and start to coat the irritating "seed" with glistening nacre. Divers periodically clean parasites from the oysters, which won't put down nacre if parasitized, and optimum production requires that lagoons not be overcrowded.

"How long does it take to produce a marketable pearl?" I inquire.

"Five years."

"How big do they get?" Dainis asks.

"The largest known is 15.7 millimetres in diameter."

"Wow!" the boys and I exclaim.

She smiles widely when we thank her. We're impressed, with the pearls and with her.

My kids and I walk a twisting gravel road that leads us through a gloomy exotic fir forest to Skyline Chalet (now Skyline Queenstown) perched on a hilltop high above Queenstown. Drizzle dogs us, and the forest is quiet except for tomtits' jingling outbursts and the rustlings made by brown creepers – small, native songbirds. We reach the chalet, discouraged after an hour of wet, boring walking and by the fact that the view I had hoped to see is obscured by cloud. However, packets of chocolate fudge and stamps from the gift shop lift Dainis's and Jānis's spirits, and my sons are intrigued by concrete luge runs in which a few people speed down the hill in one-person buggies.

Halfway down the road, we abandon the gravel and take One Mile Track for a direct, downhill plunge through beech forest bordering One Mile Creek. Mist hangs in the air, and cold stings our hands. We creep under fallen trees and skirt rock walls that slant outward and drip water onto us. Ferns and mosses cloak the wet walls, and tiny yellow beech leaves polka-dot the trail. An old cement dam and rusting pipes tell broken tales of Queenstown's earlier hydroelectric power days.

"Even though it's steeper, this trail is a lot more interesting than that road," Jānis tells me.

"Yeah," Dainis agrees.

My sons have discovered the allure of the "road less travelled."

The boys and I enter the Rydges conference room just in time to hear Vilis being introduced. We stand at the back of the darkened space, our eyes adjusting to the dim lighting. Delegates sit at tables covered with white cloths and face a brightly lit projection screen in one corner of the room.

"We are pleased to have with us today Vilis Nams from Canada," the moderator announces. "He will be speaking to us on a topic that's rather novel here in this part of the world. Grizzly bears."

Vilis launches into a description of the grizzly bear habitat use project in which he's a collaborator. His manner is easy and entertaining, drawing chuckles from the audience of South Pacific biologists who work on the opposite side of the world from where the bear study was conducted. "Grizzlies are difficult to trap," Vilis says with dry humour as he shows a slide of a heavy duty, cylindrical bear trap, "and once trapped, are rarely – if ever – caught again."

At the conclusion of the talk, Dainis, who has never before heard his father present his work, raises his eyebrows and comments, "*Hmm.* That was pretty good."

November 29

CLEAR TURQUOISE water shimmers as it laps onto Lake Wakatipu's shore. No plant grows in it. No birds ride the surface. It appears as barren as the new snow deposited on the mountains by sagging clouds last night. Today, all is clear: the sun brilliant, the lake shocking in its blueness, the peaks revealed once more. In morning's golden light, mountain forests and alpine vegetation resemble brushed velvet in shades of green and ochre topped with white lace.

Dainis and Jānis skip stones into the lake while we amble southwest on Sunshine Bay Walk to Sunshine Bay. Where rocky bluffs encroach on the beach, we follow a narrow track through scrub woodland between shore and road. Around us, the vegetation is a hodgepodge of native and introduced species. Scotch broom grows next to *mānuka* trees. Eucalyptus and cabbage trees cohabit with blackberries and lupins. Stone piles beside the trail resemble inuksuit of the Canadian Arctic. The boys and I detour around the bluffs and tramp back to the pebble beach. While skipping stones across the lake's surface, we savour the last of the fudge I bought yesterday and count the skips before the stones sink into Wakatipu's clear, shimmering depths.

CABBAGE TREE, LAKE WAKATIPU, AND SOUTHERN ALPS

In early afternoon, we meet Vilis at Rydges, and he joins us for our planned trail ride in Dart River Valley near Glenorchy, northwest of Queenstown. En route to the stables, glaciated zigzaggy Lake Wakatipu and her mountain cohorts provide what must be some of New Zealand's most spectacular scenery. Roadside lupins splash pink, purple, and yellow against the lake's sparkling blue. Cabbage trees' heads of spiky leaves resemble clumps of curved daggers hung on a backdrop of blue water and white snow. Over all, the mountains preside. Those to the south – backlit by the sun – are all sharp angles and white-crusted peaks.

The stables turn out to be a corral and several hitching posts, plus two huts for tack and helmets. Our guides for the two-hour trail ride greet us: Bonnie with long red hair and a whole lot of attitude, and Dan with dark eyes and quiet respect. We're each assigned a white crash helmet and a horse. Soon, Jānis is mounted on a dappled grey (Pete), Vilis on a tall bay (Lucky), Dainis on a smaller bay (Jingles), and I on a white-faced sorrel with three white feet (Cork). My horse looks tired, and the dried sweat on his shoulders makes me wonder how many riders Cork has already carried.

SADDLED UP

Six other riders join us: one who's never been on a horse before, two who are experienced riders, and the other three, like my family, somewhere in between. When we depart the stables in a long line, I notice a boat on the northwest tip of Lake Wakatipu and hear the faint drone of an airplane overhead. Soon, however, we leave Queenstown's thrill-o-mania behind and enter the peace of the wide Dart River Valley.

Mountains tower over us, their lower slopes forested, their upper reaches cloaked with shrubs and alpine vegetation to the snowline, which is low today due to yesterday's cold temperatures and precipitation. The river's curving, splitting, and joining tendrils decorate sand and gravel patched with willow, scrub, and grassy meadows. Water that from a distance appears blue is grey-green on closer inspection and swirls just below my boots when we cross river channels. Bonnie points out peaks within Mount Aspiring National Park: Mount Earnslaw directly ahead, and farther back to the west, Poseidon Peak. This landscape, with its long, narrow glaciated lake and steep-sided mountains, reminds me so much of Canada's Yukon Territory.

TRAIL RIDING IN DART RIVER VALLEY

When we ride into a grove of willows, resting Hereford cattle explode into motion. Our spooked horses snort and prance. "Let the horses have a look," Bonnie commands, and we pause tensely in the willows' shade. The cattle mill around us. I spot cows (a few horned), skittish calves, and a massive bull. Some animals are hidden by willows. My mind flashes back to forest surveys that took me through dense willows in another glaciated landscape. If this were the Yukon, I'd be on the lookout for grizzlies, not cattle.

After the horses settle down and we exit the willows, Dan offers a half-dozen riders the opportunity to trot. I've crooned encouraging nonsense to Cork since the ride began, and he's up for the challenge. He carries me away from my children, with whom Vilis elects to remain. At first I'm out of practice and almost lose a stirrup. However, I soon settle into regular, controlled posting as I merge with Cork's movements. From a distance, I look back to see Bonnie and her riders, small against the majesty surrounding them, and wish we all could linger in the valley.

BACK IN Queenstown, more paragliders float over the town while my family strolls downtown to buy our evening meal. As well as ubiquitous souvenir shops, the streets are lined with cafés and adventure-booking outlets. At one of the latter, we read an ad for Fly by Wire, a high-adrenaline activity that apparently involves being the passenger in a tethered airplane that flies in circles and can reach speeds of 170 kilometres per hour. All these we ignore. Instead, Vilis and I please our sons by purchasing fried chicken at KFC. While we eat outdoors, Dainis and Jānis toss bits of chicken into the air and laugh as black-billed gulls leap in a wild flutter of blurred wings and sleek, pale bodies to catch the Colonel's secret recipe.

November 30

AFTER A quick breakfast, the boys and I hurry through Queenstown's commercial district and stride uphill to the start of Queenstown Hill

Walk. As we climb the steep hill called Te Tapu Nui, "Hill of Intense Sacredness," by the Māori, we again encounter a hodgepodge of exotic and native plant species.

Partway up the hill, a wrought iron gate depicts a curve of mountain peaks, rolling waves, a large fish, a fern frond, and two birds. One of the birds is a heavy-bodied pigeon, the other perhaps a fantail. Both fly beneath a half sun. The artsy metal gate with its symbols stands like a magical doorway to the mountain realm high above Queenstown.

QUEENSTOWN VIEWED FROM QUEENSTOWN HILL

We pass through the gate into a shady Douglas fir plantation and tramp higher on the hill, pausing to read millennium interpretive displays that trace the history of human occupation in the area. We learn that Māori travelled overland in search of jade, eels, pigeons, and medicinal plants beginning in 1100 A.D. The 1860s brought Pākehā settlers and the gold rush. Tourism began to play a part in the local economy in 1939. Decades later, during the 1970s, adventure tourism took hold and led to the current tidal wave of high-adrenaline pursuits.

Beyond the plantation, we climb into an alpine realm where yellowhammers — small, yellow-tinged, sparrow-like birds — flit among rock and tussock. Rocky crags entice us to their peaks. Perched on boulders, we picnic while gazing at Lake Wakatipu's blue lightning bolt and The Remarkables mountain range stretching south in the distance. It's a view that would rival any in the world. Our spirits soar, swept aloft by the rugged beauty of our surroundings.

LAKE WAKATIPU AND THE REMARKABLES

Then we hurry down the hill, for the "Lady of the Lake" calls. During our days in Queenstown, the boys and I have many times seen the T.S.S. *Earnslaw* glide out of Frankton Arm into the lake and heard it toot its breathy blast. This afternoon, we board the Fiordland Travel tour boat, with its red-and-black smokestack vivid above a white hull. The steamer pulls out of the arm, moving faster than I expected and leaving a wake of blue, white-tipped waves as we head northwest toward Glenorchy.

Enthralled, the boys and I look down into the *Earnslaw's*

engine room, which is exposed to the view of passengers. Within it, boiler stokers shovel coal into fires that radiate heat upward. The two engines' gleaming shafts exude power in every motion. An information display proclaims the steamer's vital statistics: length 165 feet, beam 24 feet, draft 7 feet, weight 330 tons, main engines two 500-horsepower, triple-expansion, double-acting, jet-condensing steam engines.

T.S.S. *EARNSLAW* ON LAKE WAKATIPU

The T.S.S. abbreviation stands for Twin Screw Steamer. Built in Dunedin in 1911, the *Earnslaw* was dismantled and railed to Lake Wakatipu's south end, where it was reassembled and launched in 1912. The only coal-fired steamer left in New Zealand, it burns a ton of coal each hour and achieves a cruising speed of 13 knots. At various times during the *Earnslaw's* long working life, it's been a tour boat, schoolhouse, funeral parlour, wedding chapel, naval training ship, royal cruiser, and freighter of sheep, cattle, and wool.

The boys and I leave the hot engine area and walk past the steamer's lounge. Inside, a piano man belts out ragtime tunes for the entertainment of a few patrons seated at tables. We join a dozen other passengers in an open viewing area at the steamer's bow. Graceful black-billed gulls wing past the boat, and I notice there's less snow on the mountain peaks than yesterday.

A Fiordland Travel interpreter informs passengers that Lake Wakatipu is eighty-two kilometres long, three hundred to four hundred metres deep, and the third largest lake in New Zealand. The young woman, Lisa, reiterates what we learned from the displays on Queenstown Hill, that settlement and the gold rush arrived concurrently. In 1860, Walter Peak (alongside which we're cruising) was one of the first two properties settled near Queenstown. In its heyday, the mountainous station encompassed 170 000 acres, but it's since shrunk to 65 000 acres. The owners raise Merino sheep and cattle. Lisa adds that Shotover River back of Queenstown was the richest gold-mining river in the world in 1860, with over 300 000 ounces of gold mined by the end of the year.

Loud blasts of the steamer's horn compete with a cell phone's jingle, creating an incongruent juxtaposition of sounds. Brilliant sunshine plays over the lake, and scattered wisps of white cloud drift over the mountaintops. The rugged landscape seems a wilderness, but that impression is belied by exotic tree plantations, sheep stations, old mining roads, and introduced shrubs such as the Scotch broom flowering on shore.

Perhaps inspired by the ragtime piano, the reference to a gold rush era, and this tour on a steamboat, my thoughts leap to Robert Service's famous poem *The Cremation of Sam McGee*. At its opening, Service wrote of strange happenings in Yukon gold rush country. *What strange things happened beneath the southern sun when gold was extracted from Otago's mountains?*

Lisa notices that the boys and I are seated on a metal bench outside the engine room, with Dainis only a half metre away from a black line painted onto the bench. "You want to be careful," she warns. "It's hot there. It gets hotter closer to the black line."

I notice that she's sitting on a thick, insulating sweater. "It must be a hot job stoking the furnaces down there," I comment.

"Yeah. It is hot down there. Sometimes you can even feel the heat coming out the doors."

I lift my hand toward the door behind the black square and feel gusts of heat tossed at me by the wind. Soon, Jānis and I move farther from the square, our butts and legs too warm for comfort.

"My favourite part of this cruise is the ship itself," I tell the boys. "I didn't expect to like it so much, but I do. That surprised me." I hear the chug of the cylinders, the scrape of the coal shovel below, and tell Dainis and Jānis, "You're riding on a piece of history."

DURING OUR last evening in Queenstown, my family explores Queenstown Gardens. In the tidy green space, tourists flock to the Queenstown Scottish Society pipe and drum band to have photographs taken with band members. Nearby, lawn bowlers cast balls onto a level, velvet lawn. We chat with bowlers not immersed in a game and learn that the "cat" is the white ball, and that the black balls are flattened on two sides, with one side having a weight in it to help curve the shot. The players are skilful, and the game, low key. Its peacefulness is a striking contrast to the many adrenaline-rush activities we've observed in and around Queenstown.

After we leave the gardens, we cruise among buskers and night life in The Mall, a walking-only strip of shops. When I glance up, I see late sunlight painting gold dust onto the mountains across Lake Wakatipu.

It's a fitting end to our time in Queenstown. Tomorrow, we'll return to Lincoln, and two weeks from today, we'll embark on the next phase of our New Zealand adventure. More than a third of the way through our time in this country, we'll finally immerse ourselves in Vilis's stoat research on North Island. Our mid-summer will be spent in a subtropical rainforest on the Central Volcanic Plateau, where wild cries of kiwi split the night.

GLOSSARY

Aotearoa – Māori name for New Zealand; means "Land of the Long White Cloud" or "Land of the Long Daylight"

haka – war dance, with chanting

harakeke, kōrari – flax, a robust clumping plant with straplike leaves

hoki – a marine fish found in New Zealand and southern Australian waters

horoeka – lancewood

horopito – pepper tree

iwi – tribe

kākā – forest parrot

kākāpō – flightless, nocturnal parrot

kākāriki – red- or yellow-crowned parakeet

kānuka – shrub or small tree with stringy bark and small, flat leaves

kauri – conifer tree; among the world's largest trees

kea – alpine parrot

kete – basket

kia ora – hello or thank you

kiore – rat

kōtuku – white heron

kōwhai – tree with small, paired leaves and yellow flowers; New Zealand's national tree

kūmara – yellow-fleshed sweet potato

kurī – dog

korimako, also *makomako, titimoko* – bellbird

mahinga kai – garden

mānuka – shrub with small, flat leaves

matai – tall conifer tree; recently peeled bark creates rounded red
  scars on trunk

mere – short, flat club

moa – extinct flightless bird

nīkau – palm tree

ongaonga – tree nettle

pā – hilltop fortress; stockaded village

Pākehā – European or Caucasian

patu – bat used as a weapon

pāua – abalone

ponga – silver fern

pouakai, also *hokio,* **Haast eagle** – extinct giant eagle

pounamu, also **greenstone** – New Zealand jade; nephrite

puawānanga – clematis

pūkeko – marsh bird with blue-black plumage; swamp hen

rimu – tall conifer tree with weeping twigs

tapu – sacred

taro – tropical plant with edible starchy tubers

tī kōuka, also **cabbage tree** – tree with branched crown having
  clumps of long, pointed leaves

tuatara – ancient lizard

tūī – blackish-brown songbird with two white feather tufts dangling
  from throat

waka – canoe

waka taua – war canoe

whēkī – stout tree fern with a thick skirt of dead leaves

REFERENCES AND NOTES

[1] Keith Sinclair. (2000). *A History of New Zealand*. Auckland: Penguin Books. pp. 14, 19, 29-31.

[2] Ministry for Primary Industries *Manatū Ahu Matua*. (Accessed 6-Mar-2015). "Travel and Recreation: Items to Declare." http://www.mpi.govt.nz/travel-and-recreation/arriving-in-new-zealand/items-to-declare/.

[3] Department of Conservation *Te Papa Atawhai*. (Accessed 6-Mar-2015). "Animal Pests – Stoats." http://www.doc.govt.nz/conservation/threats-and-impacts/animal-pests/animal-pests-a-z/stoats/.

[4] Department of Conservation *Te Papa Atawhai*. (Accessed 6-Mar-2015). "Birds – Kiwi." http://www.doc.govt.nz/conservation/native-animals/birds/birds-a-z/kiwi/.

[5] Craig Gillies. (Accessed 6-Mar-2015). "Controlling Mustelids for Conservation in New Zealand," pp. 3, 11. Department of Conservation *Te Papa Atawhai*. http://www.kiwisforkiwi.org/wp-content/uploads/2012/09/Controlling_Mustelids_2007_CraigGillies.pdf.

[6] Laura Harper, Tony Mudd, and Paul Whitfield. (1998). *New Zealand: The Rough Guide*. London: The Rough Guides. pp. 478, 480.

[7] Carl Walrond. (Accessed 6-Mar-2015). "Natural Environment – Geography and geology." *Te Ara* – the Encyclopedia of New Zealand. http://www.teara.govt.nz/en/natural-environment/page-1; GNS Science *Te Pū Ao*, (Accessed 6-Mar-2015). "Earthquakes at a Plate Boundary." http://www.gns.cri.nz/Home/Learning/Science-Topics/Earthquakes/Earthquakes-at-a-Plate-Boundary.

[8] Walrond, http://www.teara.govt.nz/en/natural-environment/page-1.

[9] Thomas D. Isern. (2002). "Companions, Stowaways, Imperialists, Invaders: Pests and Weeds in New Zealand." In *Environmental Histories of New Zealand*, edited by Eric Pawson and Tom Brooking. South Melbourne: Oxford University Press. p. 233; Narena Olliver. (Accessed 6-Mar-2015). "Starling." New Zealand Birds. http://www.nzbirds.com/birds/starlings.html.

[10] Isern, pp. 241-243; Q. Paynter, A. H. Gourlay, C. A. Rolando, and M. S. Watt. (2012). "Dispersal of the Scotch broom gall mite *Aceria genistae*: implications for biocontrol." New Zealand Plant Protection 65: 81–84.

[11] Simon Nathan and Bruce Hayward. (Accessed 6-Mar-2015). "Building stone – Igneous rocks." *Te Ara* – the Encyclopedia of New Zealand. http://www.teara.govt.nz/en/building-stone/page-4.

[12] Peggy Dunstan. (1981). *A Fistful of Summer.* Christchurch: Whitcoulls Publishers. pp. 10-13.

[13] Atholl Anderson. (2002). "A Fragile Plenty: Pre-European Māori and the New Zealand Environment." In *Environmental Histories of New Zealand*, edited by Eric Pawson and Tom Brooking. South Melbourne: Oxford University Press. p. 34.

[14] Department of Conservation *Te Papa Atawhai*. (Accessed 6-Mar-2015). "Animal pests – Hedgehogs." http://www.doc.govt.nz/conservation/threats-and-impacts/animal-pests/animal-pests-a-z/hedgehogs/.

[15] Department of Conservation *Te Papa Atawhai*. (Accessed 6-Mar-2015). "Bats/pekapeka." http://www.doc.govt.nz/conservation/native-animals/bats/.

[16] Isern, pp. 233-245.

[17] Judith Bassett, Keith Sinclair, and Marcia Stenson. (1985). *The Story of New Zealand.* Auckland: Reed Methuen. p. 12.

[18] John Dawson and Rob Lucas. (2000). *Nature Guide to the New Zealand Forest.* Auckland: Random House New Zealand. pp. 10-11.

[19] Sinclair, pp. 14-19; Anderson, pp. 27-29.

[20] Evelyn Stokes. (2002). "Contesting Resources – Māori, Pākehā, and a Tenurial Revolution." In *Environmental Histories of New Zealand*, edited by Eric Pawson and Tom Brooking. South Melbourne: Oxford University Press, pp. 37-38, 41-43; Anderson, p. 32; Kerry-Jayne Wilson. (Accessed 7-Mar-2015) "Land birds – overview – Extinct, endangered and threatened species." *Te Ara* – the Encyclopedia of New Zealand. http://www.teara.govt.nz/en/land-birds-overview/page-4.

[21] Gillies, pp. 10-11; Kay Griffiths. (Accessed 7-Mar-2015). "Stoat Control in New Zealand: A Review." Wildlife Management Report Number 108, University of Otago. (1999). p. 8, 11. http://theconservationcompany.co.nz/pdf/stoat thesis.pdf; Department of Conservation *Te Papa Atawhai*. (Accessed 7-Mar-2015). "Animal pests – Stoats." http://www.doc.govt.nz/conservation/threats-and-impacts/animal-pests/animal-pests-a-z/stoats/.

[22] Kevin Krajick. (2005). "Winning the war against island invaders." *Science,* 2 December 2005, volume 310, no. 5753, pp. 1410-1413.

[23] Bassett, Sinclair, and Stenson, pp. 9-11; Dawson and Lucas, pp. 11, 286; Anderson, pp. 27-28; Wikipedia. (Accessed 6-Mar-2015). "Moa." http://en.wikipedia.org/wiki/Moa.

[24] Sinclair, p. 12-13; Basset, Sinclair, and Stenson, p. 12.

[25] Edmund Bohan. (1997). *New Zealand - The Story So Far. A Short History*. London: Harper Collins. p. 10; Basset, Sinclair, and Stenson, p. 13.

[26] Basset, Sinclair, and Stenson, p. 13.

[27] A. E. Jackman, S. M. Mason, and G. H. Densem. (Accessed 7-Mar-2015). "An Environmental Plan for Lincoln Village." Landscape Architecture Section, Horticultural Department, Lincoln College, New Zealand Study No. 15. (1973). https://researcharchive.lincoln.ac.nz/bitstream/10182/5134/1/LincolnT ownship.pdf ; Mark Pickering. (1999). "Bridle Path and Mount Cavendish." In *The Port Hills: a guide to the walking tracks on the Port Hills*. Christchurch: Mark Pickering, pp. 28-29.

[28] Anderson, p. 31.

[29] Olliver. (Accessed 7-Mar-2015). "Pouakai, the Haast eagle." http://www.nzbirds.com/birds/haasteagle.html; (e)Science News (Accessed 7-Mar-2015). "Extinct, Giant Eagle Was a Fearsome Predator." http://esciencenews.com/sources/newswise.scinews/2009/09/11/extinc t.giant.eagle.was.a.fearsome.predator.

[30] *Ibid.*

[31] Sinclair, pp. 13-14; Basset, Sinclair, and Stenson, pp. 12-13; Anderson, p. 26.

[32] Anderson, p. 25; Basset, Sinclair, and Stenson, p. 14.

[33] Bohan, pp. 13-15; Sinclair, p. 15; Basset, Sinclair, and Stenson, pp. 13- 14.

[34] Sinclair, pp. 14-20.

[35] *Ibid*, p. 29-30.

[36] Sinclair, pp. 29-31; Basset, Sinclair, and Stenson, pp. 18-19; Department of Conservation *Te Papa Atawhai*. (1998). "Abel Tasman Parkmap." Historical note for Golden Bay reads "Golden Bay – originally called Murderer's Bay ('Moordaerer's Baay') by Abel Tasman the name was changed to Massacre Bay and then to Coal Bay before it was given its present name."

[37] Sinclair, pp. 30-33.

[38] Bassett, Sinclair, and Stenson, p. 20; John Wilson. (Accessed 7-Mar-2015). "European discovery of New Zealand – Cook's three voyages." *Te Ara –* the Encyclopedia of New Zealand. http://www.TeAra.govt.nz/en/european-discovery-of-new-zealand/page-5.

[39] Sinclair, p. 31; Bohan, pp. 16-17; P. A. Tomory. (Accessed 7-Mar-2015). "*Captain James Cook: his Artists and Draughtsmen*." Auckland City Art Gallery,

October-December, 1964; biographical notes of artists featured in the exhibition of "some of the paintings and drawings, by Cook, his artists and draughtsmen, made during or consequently to the three voyages." http://www.aucklandartgallery.com/media/335251/cat69.pdf.

[40] Bassett, Sinclair, and Stenson, pp. 20-25; Bohan, pp. 16- 17; Sinclair, pp. 31-32.

[41] Bassett, Sinclair, and Stenson, pp. 20-25; Bohan, pp. 16- 17; Sinclair, pp. 32.

[42] Bohan, p. 17.

[43] Jock Phillips. (Accessed 7-Mar-2015). "Bridges and tunnels – Rail tunnels." *Te Ara* – the Encyclopedia of New Zealand. http://www.TeAra.govt.nz/en/bridges-and-tunnels/page-5; "Bridges and tunnels – Road and utility tunnels." *Te Ara* – the Encyclopedia of New Zealand. http://www.teara.govt.nz/en/bridges-and-tunnels/page-6.

[44] Christchurch City Libraries *Ngā Kete Wānanga-o-Ōtautahi*. (Accessed 7-Mar-2015). "The First Four Ships." http://my.christchurchcitylibraries.com/the-first-four-ships/.

[45] Summit Road Society. (Accessed 7-Mar-2015). "Harry Ell and the Summit Road." http://www.summitroadsociety.org.nz/history.htm.

[46] Sinclair, pp. 34-35; Bassett, Sinclair, and Stenson, pp. 28-31; Bohan, pp. 17-19.

[47] Sinclair, pp. 34-35; Bohan, pp. 18-19; Basset, Sinclair, and Stenson, p. 29-31.

[48] Basset, Sinclair, and Stenson, pp. 31-32; Sinclair, pp. 35-36; Stokes, pp. 41-43.

[49] Eileen McSaveney and Simon Nathan. (Accessed 7-Mar-2015). "Geology – overview – New Zealand reborn." *Te Ara* – the Encyclopedia of New Zealand. http://www.TeAra.govt.nz/en/photograph/8382/banks-peninsula-extinct-volcanoes.

[50] Department of Conservation *Te Papa Atawhai*. (Accessed 7-Mar-2015). "Banks Peninsula reserves." http://www.doc.govt.nz/parks-and-recreation/places-to-visit/canterbury/christchurch-and-banks-peninsula/banks-peninsula-reserves/features/.

[51] Simon E. Jolly, Phil E. Cowan, and Janine A. Duckworth. (Accessed 7-Mar-2015). "Research to Develop Contraceptive Control of Brushtail Possums in New Zealand." *Contraception in Wildlife Management*. Paper 12. (1993). http://digitalcommons.unl.edu/nwrccontraception/12; Isern, pp.235-237.

[52] Dawson and Lucas, pp. 41, 123-126.

[53] *Purnell's Illustrated Encyclopedia of Modern Weapons and Warfare*. (1978). "Camel, Sopwith." Part 26. p. 510-513.

[54] Harper, Mudd, and Whitfield, p. 497.

[55] Mark Pickering. (1999). "Godley Head." In *The Port Hills: a guide to the walking tracks on the Port Hills*. Christchurch: Mark Pickering. p. 34.

[56] *Ibid*, pp. 34-35.

[57] John Keast. (2000). "Lights, camera, action…" *The Press*, Saturday, September 16, 2000. p. 1.

[58] Christchurch City Libraries *Ngā Kete Wānanga-o-Ōtautahi*. (Accessed 7-Mar-2015). "Te Waihora – Lake Ellesmere."
http://my.christchurchcitylibraries.com/ti-kouka-whenua/te-waihora/;
John Wilson. (Accessed 7-Mar-2015). "Canterbury places – Ellesmere district." *Te Ara* – the Encyclopedia of New Zealand.
http://www.teara.govt.nz/en/canterbury-places/page-16.

[59] Mona Anderson. (1988). *A River Rules My Life*. Auckland: Beckett Publishing. pp. 11- 27.

[60] Basset, Sinclair, and Stenson, p. 23.

[61] *Ibid*, pp. 12-16; Bohan, pp.10-15; Sinclair, pp. 24-25.

[62] Basset, Sinclair, and Stenson, pp. 9-10; Witi Ihimaera and Tim Plant. (1998). *This is New Zealand*. Auckland: Reed Books. pp. 13-14.

[63] Basil Keane. (Accessed 7-Mar-2015). "Pounamu – jade or greenstone." *Te Ara* – the Encyclopedia of New Zealand.
http://www.teara.govt.nz/en/pounamu-jade-or-greenstone.

[64] *Ibid*.

[65] Isern, p. 234-235.

[66] Basset, Sinclair, and Stenson, pp. 32-39; Bohan, pp. 20-21.

[67] Sinclair, pp. 26, 39-41; John Miller. (1958). *Early Victorian New Zealand: A Study of Racial Problems and Social Attitudes 1839-1852*. London: Oxford University Press, pp. 14-19.

[68] Sinclair, pp. 41.

[69] Sinclair, pp. 26, 201.

[70] *Ibid*, pp. 35, 41.

[71] *Ibid*, pp. 41, 48, 54; Miller, pp. 26, 48-49.

[72] Miller, pp. 48-96; Sinclair, p. 78-85.

[73] Sinclair, p. 42.

[74] Sinclair, p. 41. (Quoted by kind permission.)

[75] Miller, p. 21.

[76] Sinclair, p. 36.

77 Sinclair, p. 42; Basset, Sinclair, and Stenson, p. 33; Bohan, p. 20.

78 Bohan, pp. 20-21; Sinclair, pp. 42, 52.

79 Isern, p. 233.

80 Sinclair, pp. 118-120.

81 Phyllis Johnston. (1982). *Black Boots and Buttonhooks.* Wellington: Price Milburn and Company Limited. pp. 7-8, 104.

82 Dawson and Lucas, p. 50.

83 Keri Hulme. (1985). *The Bone People.* Baton Rouge: Louisiana State University Press. p. 5. (Quoted by kind permission.)

84 Christopher Moore. (2000). "Worst storm in decade hits Canterbury." *The Press,* Christchurch. Friday, October 13, 2000. p. 3.

85 Walrond. (Accessed 7-Mar-2015). "Natural environment." *Te Ara* – the Encyclopedia of New Zealand. http://www.TeAra.govt.nz/en/natural-environment.

86 Interpretive displays within the reconstructed entrance to Blackburn Mine.

87 Judith Armstrong. (Accessed 7-Mar-2015). "The Challenges of farming in Mid-Canterbury, Part 4: Farming changes in Dorie since 1990 – problems with water, new dairy farms." *NZine,* October 13, 2003. http://www.nzine.co.nz/features/armstrong4.html.

88 Harper, Mudd, and Whitfield, p. xi.

89 Armstrong, http://www.nzine.co.nz/features/armstrong4.html.

90 Sinclair, p. 319.

91 Eric Pawson and Tom Brooking. (2002). "Introduction." In *Environmental Histories of New Zealand,* edited by Eric Pawson and Tom Brooking. South Melbourne: Oxford University Press. p. 4.

92 Mark Pickering. (2000). "Peninsula Summit Walking Tracks." In *Banks Peninsula: a guide to the walks and beaches of Banks Peninsula.* Christchurch: Mark Pickering. pp. 13-14.

93 Bassett, Sinclair, and Stenson, pp. 42-43.

94 Miller, p. 1.

95 *Ibid,* p. 4.

96 *Ibid,* quoting Edward Gibbon Wakefield, p. 9.

97 *Ibid.*

98 Basset, Sinclair, and Stenson, pp. 42-43; Sinclair, pp. 51-70.

[99] Basset, Sinclair, and Stenson, pp. 43-47.

[100] Sinclair, p. 120.

[101] F. M. (Jock) Brookfield. (2006). *Waitangi and Indigenous Rights: Revolution, Law, and Legitimation.* Auckland: Auckland University Press. p. 12.

[102] Sinclair, pp. 347-349.

[103] GNS Science *Te Pū Ao.* (Accessed 7-Mar-2015). "New Zealand Earthquakes." http://www.gns.cri.nz/Home/Learning/Science-Topics/Earthquakes/New-Zealand-Earthquakes; "Plate Collision in NZ." http://www.gns.cri.nz/Home/Learning/Science-Topics/Earthquakes/Earthquakes-at-a-Plate-Boundary/Plate-Collision-in-NZ; "Where were New Zealand's largest earthquakes?" http://www.gns.cri.nz/Home/Learning/Science-Topics/Earthquakes/New-Zealand-Earthquakes/Where-were-NZs-largest-earthquakes.

[104] *The New Zealand Herald.* (Accessed 7-Mar-2015). "Christchurch earthquake – quick facts." Tuesday, February 22, 2011. http://www.nzherald.co.nz/nz/news/article.cfm?c_id=1&objectid=1070 8024.

[105] GeoNet. (Accessed 7-Mar-2015). "Quake statistics." http://www.geonet.org.nz/quakes/statistics.

[106] Tim Stoddard. (Accessed 7-Mar-2015). "Kiwis saving kiwis." *Zoogoer* 28(6), November/December 1999. http://www.archive-edu-2012.com/open-archive/623754/2012-11-11/1d3efc08d8d19047ffd354183f071425.

[107] "Fireworks extravaganza set to light the sky." *The Press,* Christchurch. Saturday, November 4, 2000.

[108] James Sales. (2005). "The endangered kiwi: a review." *Folia Zoologica* 54(1-2):1-20.

[109] *Ibid.*

[110] Bohan, p.13.

[111] Sinclair, p. 73-74; Harper, Mudd, and Whitfield, p. 515.

[112] Andrew Crowe. (1998). *Which Native Tree? A Simple Guide to the Identification of New Zealand Native Trees.* Auckland: Penguin Books (NZ) Ltd. p. 45.

[113] Charlie Janes. (1993). *Time for a Brew.* Auckland: Reed Books; (1998). *Possum on a Cold Tin Roof.* Auckland: Reed Books.

[114] Andrew Crowe. (1994). *Which Native Forest Plant? A Simple Guide to the Identification of New Zealand Native Forest Shrubs, Climbers and Flowers.* Auckland: Penguin Books (NZ) Ltd. p. 36.

[115] Crowe, *Which Native Tree?* p. 24.

[116] Crowe, *Which Native Forest Plant?* p. 60.

[117] Harper, Mudd, and Whitfield, p. xi.

[118] *Ibid.*

[119] Margaret Hall. (1993) *Swag and Tucker.* Dunedin: McIndoe.

[120] Isaac Theatre Royal. (Accessed 7-Mar-2015). "Theatre History." http://isaactheatreroyal.co.nz/our-history/theatre-history/.

[121] Crowe, *Which Native Forest Plant?* p. 25.

[122] Janet Frame. (1957). *Owls Do Cry.* Christchurch: Pegasus Press. ©Janet Frame Literary Trust. (Quoted by kind permission.)

[123] New Zealand Book Council *Te Kaunihera Pukapuka o Aotearoa.* (Accessed 7-Mar-2015). "Frame, Janet." http://www.bookcouncil.org.nz/writers/profiles/frame, janet.

[124] Sinclair, pp. 367-368.

[125] Tourism New Zealand. (Accessed 7-Mar-2015). "Central Otago." http://www.newzealand.com/travel/media/topic-index/nz-regions/central-otago.cfm.

[126] Carl Walrond. (Accessed 7-Mar-2015). "Gold and gold mining – Otago." *Te Ara* – the Encyclopedia of New Zealand. http://www.teara.govt.nz/en/gold-and-gold-mining/page-3; "Gold and gold mining – Miners." http://www.teara.govt.nz/en/gold-and-gold-mining/page-9; Wikipedia. (Accessed 7-Mar-2015). "Otago Gold Rush." http://en.wikipedia.org/wiki/Otago_Gold_Rush.

INDEX

11656862R00148

Printed in Great Britain
by Amazon.co.uk, Ltd.,
Marston Gate.